Take Your Band Saw Box to the Next Level

Take Your Band Saw Box to the Next Level

Dave Grabarczyk

WoodenCreations.org

Please Read Safety Notice and Disclaimer

I've learned from personal experience that woodworking can be and is dangerous. Always use caution when working around power equipment. Wear goggles and use a push stick to keep fingers away from moving blades. Don't wear loose clothing or jewelry that can be caught in equipment.

Read each tools' instruction manual and follow the safety guidelines provided.

NOTE: Many of the pictures in this book have the safety guards removed to show better clarity of the operation that is pictured. In most instances the tools were turned off for the picture when it was taken. The author does not condone the removing of the safety guards.

The author has reviewed each step and has tried to make them as clear and as accurate as possible. Due to the variety of skill levels of those who may read this book, the author or publisher assumes no responsibility for any accidents, injuries, damages or other loss that may arise from working on the projects contained within.

Product Disclaimer

The tools and products pictured in this book are ones that are used by the author. No financial compensation has been exchanged for their inclusion and no specific endorsement has been made.

Metric Conversion Chart

To convert	To	Multiply By
Inches	Centimeters	2.54
Centimeters	Inches	0.39370
		Or 0.4

Library of Congress Control Number 2021914211

ISBN: 978-1-7371696-3-5 (Ingram)

Additional ISBN identifiers

ISBN: 978-1-7371696-5-9 (BN)

ISBN: 978-1-7371696-4-2 (BN)

Publisher: WoodenCreations.org / Perrysburg, Ohio

Edited by Dave Grabarczyk

Cover Design by Dave Grabarczyk

Photographs by Dave Grabarczyk

Sketch Design Assistance by Sidney Parkhill

For questions or more information contact Dave Grabarczyk at:

daveswoodencreations@yahoo.com

Dedication

To my wife Marge and my daughters, Andrea and Jennifer who have had to deal with the noise, dust and smell over the years as I pursued my hobby while working in the basement of our home.

Acknowledgements

My special thanks go to master box builder Dave Ross from Bryan, Ohio who very generously allowed me into his shop many years ago to show me some of his box techniques that I have now incorporated into my designs.

To my son-in-law, Keith Franklin, who was the one that suggested I write this book.

To the Toledo Craftsman's Guild for over 35 years of support.

To the many Craft and Fine Art Show jurors and directors who allowed me to participate in their shows over the years.

To my many customers who have purchased my boxes either for themselves or for gifts for others. I wouldn't be doing this if it wasn't for your support!

Contents

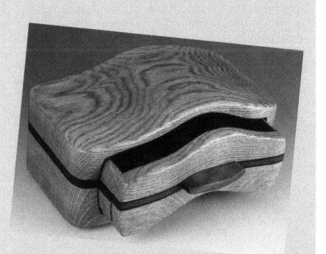

Contents

Introduction
Functional Art

You may have seen several band saw boxes at a craft or an art show at some time. You have probably seen patterns for them in woodworking books or magazines. You probably thought that they were pretty cool and that you would like to make some as they would make for great gifts for your family or friends. You may have even thought that you could sell a few yourself. Well, you can do all of those things because that is what I did!

I was selling oak shelving, coat racks, small tables and traditional valet boxes at area craft shows for many years. I saw my first band saw boxes in the book "Building Beautiful Boxes with Your Band Saw" by Lois Keener Ventura and I too thought that they were pretty cool, so I made a few as gifts. After giving many away, I decided to add them to the items I sold at the craft shows. I've since discontinued selling the functional household items and now sell the band saw boxes that I make at area art shows. And yes, people do think that they are pretty cool.

Band saw boxes have been around for many years I like to call them "functional art". They not only serve a purpose for storing jewelry, keepsakes, and small personal items, but they look great as a decorative work of art that belongs on display.

My first band saw was a Swiss made Inca euro model 260 that I purchased over 35 years ago from master woodworker and band saw book author Mark Duginske at a woodworking show in Columbus, Ohio. He was the Midwestern Sales rep for Injecta Machinery Corporation at that time. I still have his business card attached to my saw manual. The saw was exceptionally well made and featured a direct drive motor. It had a 6 inch cutting capacity. I made my first band saw box on that saw, much to the amazement of my family.

Since that time I have purchased two other band saws that I use for making my band saw boxes. However, I still have that first Inca model which I occasionally use as a backup. It still runs great!

The fun part of making a band saw box is cutting out the drawers and the box profile. This is where you will see your project begin to take shape and you can envision what the final product will look like. That should be enough to put a smile on your face.

That task is completed rather quickly.

A few years ago, my daughter and her husband gave me a band saw box book for a Christmas present.

My son-in-law said, "why don't you write your own book", I chuckled at that suggestion, but I did take a few pictures the next time that I made a batch of boxes and set them aside for a couple of years.

When the pandemic hit in 2020, I found that I had a lot of extra time on my hands, so I pulled out those old pictures and started working on writing a few chapters. I eventually made another batch of boxes, took new pictures and I have used them in writing this book.

The majority of my boxes are similar in design but are made in different sizes. I like to call it a contemporary design because it has two small arcs with gentle waves like that found on a flowing body of water on a calm day.

A lot of the focus of the book will not be on the box profile itself, but on the configuration of the drawers. You are basically starting with a block of wood. There are literally hundreds of configurations that can be done with it. Not every box will be perfect, but that imperfection often adds to the charm of the finished product.

The first few chapters will deal with tools, wood selection, preparation, design, and making a basic band saw box. The middle chapters will deal with taking that box to the next level by showing you how to add a pull-out tray, a side mini-drawer or a back hidden mini-drawer. Additional chapters will show you how to increase the functionality of the box by splitting the drawer and adding many more sectional compartments.

There will be a chapter on sanding and a look at finishing your box. However, a book this size can't possibly cover every aspect of selecting the finish you should use, as finishing is a personal choice. There are plenty of books available on that topic for you to look at.

The appendix will have a number of pattern templates. There will be drawer configuration suggestions along with both a top and front view look of many of the drawer options.

Be sure to read the numerous tips and note boxes that are provided. They provide insight into special situations with some of the boxes.

The designs are just a start, improvise, find an easier way to make them, come up with your own patterns that will make your box as beautiful and unique as I think these are. Make them as gifts or to sell. The choice will be yours!

If you learn something new from this book that you didn't know before, then my task as a writer has been successful.

Dave grabarczyk

Taking the time to be creative is
one of the best uses of your time!

Chapter 1-
Tools

Do I need a lot of tools to make a band saw box?

Not really! If you have some basic tools, a band saw, a few clamps, lots of sandpaper and a palm sander then you can probably make a band saw box with a little effort. However, the more boxes you make, the easier and quicker they can be created with the right power tools.

Band Saws

The size of band saw you choose will be determined by the size of band saw boxes or other projects that you plan to make.

Most home based woodworkers will usually choose between the 12" or 14" band saw with a fence. The larger the size, the more capacity you will have in height or depth of cut from the table to the top roller blades. This will also determine the width of cut, most often referred to as the throat, which is the distance between the blade to the support arm. A minimum of 6" in height should suffice for most band saw boxes.

Search Google for band saw specifications and reviews for more information to help you decide the right one for you as there are numerous models on the market to choose from.

Band Saw Blades

Band saw blades come in different widths, styles and number of teeth per inch (TPI).

Wider blades will give you a straighter cut and are good for resawing and cutting off the backs of larger band saw boxes.

Narrower blades will cut a smaller radius and will be the blade that you will use the most.

The more teeth per inch will give you a smoother cut, but can clog trying to remove the sawdust.

My go to blade is a regular 3/16" blade at 10TPI, others prefer the 3/16" with 4TPI. I'll also use a 1/2" blade at 6TPI for straight line cutting and for larger wavy cuts.

Band saw blades will leave saw marks and will require sanding no matter what the TPI.

Chart shows estimated radius cut.

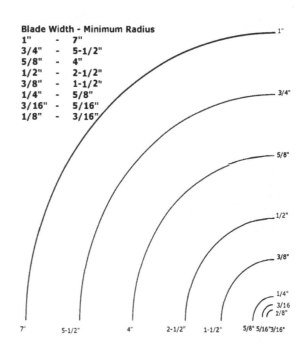

Blade Width	-	Minimum Radius
1"	-	7"
3/4"	-	5-1/2"
5/8"	-	4"
1/2"	-	2-1/2"
3/8"	-	1-1/2"
1/4"	-	5/8"
3/16"	-	5/16"
1/8"	-	3/16"

Clamps

Pipe, F bar or C clamps of different sizes are an essential tool in making band saw boxes with the F bar clamps being the one used the most often. I've learned that you can never have enough clamps, so plan to have plenty on hand.

You don't need a lot of expensive ones, as even the inexpensive ones, while not as sturdy, will suffice for clamping up your parts.

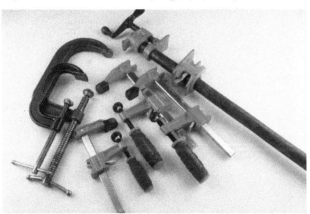

The Basics

Some may not consider the items below as tools, but some are necessary everyday shop items and others are optional accessories.

You will need a ruler for measuring, pencils or a marker for drawing patterns along with plenty of brushes for gluing.

A square will be needed for tool set up and for checking the box blocks for squareness. The combination square will be used for marking reference and parallel lines to the edge of your box.

A center ruler and a French curve are optional items, but will help in laying out the box designs and the drawer patterns. The contour gauge is beneficial in tracing handles for the contoured box drawers.

Glue

You can't make a band saw box without it.

Sandpaper

We only think about sandpaper when we need to sand something smooth. Sandpaper comes in a variety of materials, backings and grits. You will probably use a little of each kind as you move up the grits from 100, 120, 150, 180 and higher.

Initial rough sanding can be accomplished with 100 or even 120 grit. I find that 80 grit paper is too rough. Follow that up with 150 grit. I prefer cloth backed aluminum oxide for the rough sanding as it can take a beating whether by hand or on a machine .

Move up to 180 grit garnet cabinet paper to prep for staining. Follow that with higher grit silicon carbide paper between finish coats.

Sanding sponges are quite useful in softening the edges and following contours.

Automotive detail type sandpaper pads come in higher grits and work well between coats of finish.

Power Tools

It is feasible that the band saw is the only power tool that you will need to make a band saw box if you are willing to spend a lot of time hand sanding.

The box profile, the drawers and the handles are all cut on the band saw. You can even rip and crosscut your stock using a fence and miter gauge to make the box block using just the band saw, but other power tools make the job so much easier.

A planer will be needed if wood is purchased in the rough. A table saw can be used to rip wider boards or crosscut boards to size using a miter gauge. A joiner will be used to smooth out the rough edges from the table saw cut and smoothing out the glued up box blocks. A miter saw is the ideal tool to use to cut numerous pieces to the same length.

Sanding Equipment

Hand power sanders are be an essential tool to use when making band saw boxes.

The belt sander can be used to rough sand box blocks smooth prior to cutting.

The palm and orbital sanders are ideal to use on flat areas prior to finish sanding by hand.

Optional Sanding Equipment

A majority of my box prep and rough sanding is completed on a stationary oscillating edge belt sander using 100 grit paper. It handles the box blocks easily and the roller end is ideal for sanding the contours of a box. It has seen a lot of use over the years.

Not everyone needs a large belt sander. There are several smaller benchtop or floor models that also have a disc on the side that will adequately handle rough sanding.

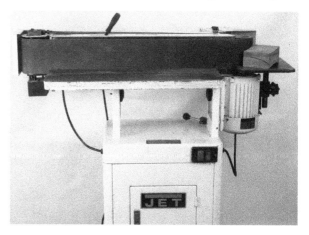

Another optional power sander is an oscillating spindle sander. It is a nice tool to have when sanding curves. The sander works by moving a round hard roller drum with a sanding sleeve attached up and down while rotating at the same time. This action creates a smooth edge without burn marks that can be caused by using a drum sander on a drill press.

The round sleeves are easily changed and come in different diameters and grits usually starting at 1/2 inch up to 3 inches or more.

13

A pneumatic or inflatable drum sander is a luxury tool to have. It is for the woodworker who likes to have all of the woodworking toys or the serious hobbyist who wants to do things easier.

Unlike hard rubber drum rollers, the hardness of the inflatable drum can be controlled by how much air pressure is used. Use a softer drum with less pressure when sanding the rounded edges of a box. Add air for a harder drum when sanding curves and flat areas. The drums are available in different diameters.

Besides the bench models, there are inflatable models that you can use with your portable drill, drill press or lathe.

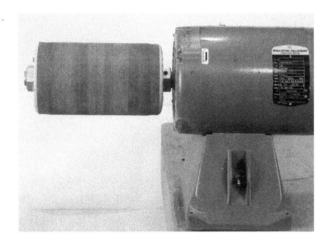

Flap sanders are generally not found in many home work shops. A flap sander has strips of sandpaper usually backed up by synthetic or natural bristles. The flap wheels are flexible enough to conform around contours and works well at softening the square edges without the use of a router. The flaps do come in different grits.

Besides the stationary models, you can find some flaps that will fit on a portable drill and others that will work with a drill press.

Pin Nailer

I am sure that you are wondering why I included a pin nailer as an optional tool in a band saw box book.

Some of the drawers you will find in the later chapters have numerous parts. A 1/2" pin pinned on the back side aids greatly in keeping the parts aligned for gluing.

Digital Angle Gauge

It is important to have accurate tool set ups when making band saw boxes. In the past we would normally use a square for checking the perpendicular alignment of the blade and the fence to the table.

A digital angel gauge improves on your ability to have highly accurate blade and fence set ups with the band saw and other tools including the jointer fence.

This is not a definitive list of tools that you may find helpful in making a band saw box. Other tools include a router, chisels, miter gauge, caliper, safety goggles, push sticks, thickness sander and even a copy machine.

I'm sure that you will find a few more not listed yourself.

Chapter 2-
Wood Selection

There are many kinds of woods out there, so which ones do I choose? Hardwoods work best on band saw boxes. There is a large variety of domestic hardwoods to choose from where I live in the Midwest, so the majority of my boxes are made out of ash, white oak, walnut, cherry, and maple. Depending on where you live, you might be limited to what kind of wood is generally available in your area so that may be the type of wood you use for your band saw box.

Retailers - You can pick up some hardwoods in your local big box store or maybe a local woodworker's supply store, but you will be limited to the variety of woods and thicknesses that they may have on hand.

The benefit by buying at one of these outlets is that the wood has been surface planed and edged to standard dimensions and are usually free of knots and defects. Another benefit is that you can buy some pieces of wood, start cutting, and begin gluing up your band saw blocks rather quickly. These boards are generally sold by the lineal foot. You may also be able to pick up some thin pieces of wood such as 1/4 inch or 1/2 inch that are ready to use too.

I have also bought some of my wood from mail order outlets and eBay when I was looking for something in particular to use. Do a Google search and you will find lots of places that will ship you wood directly.

Sample stack of types of 1/4" woods that I use in many of my boxes. From top to bottom: wenge; ash; purpleheart; maple; bloodwood; walnut; white oak

Sawmill Lumber - most hardwoods purchased from a sawmill are in the "rough" and are not consumer ready to be used. They are usually sold random width and random length. They will need to be surfaced planed and edged to the dimensions that you want them at. All sawmills will generally plane and edge one or two sides for you at an additional cost. Hardwoods are generally labeled and sold by the quarter inch in the rough as this chart shows.

Rough Size	Nominal Size	Surfaced 2 sides
4/4 inch	1 inch	13/16 inch
5/4 inch	1 1/4 inch	1 1/16 inch
6/4 inch	1/1/2 inch	1 5/16 inch
8/4 inch	2 inches	1 3/4 inch

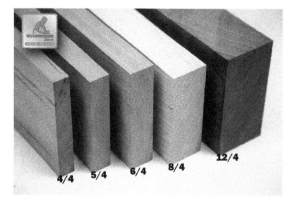

https://www.woodworkerssource.com - No copyright infringement is intended.

15

Sawmill hardwoods also come in different grades based on the size and number of clear pieces that can be obtained from a board when it is cut up to be used in making a product. They are usually labeled as: Firsts and Seconds (FAS) which has @83% minimum clear cutting; Select (SEL) also @83% clear; No 1 Common (1C) @66% clear cutting.

Generally when you buy Select and Better boards from a sawmill you will receive a mixture of firsts and seconds and select boards. These boards are sold by the board foot (12 inches long x 12 inches wide x 1 inch thick). For example a board that is 8 inches wide by 6 feet long x 1 inch thick is 4 board feet; the same board at 1 1/4 inches thick would be 5 board feet. You will find free and easy to use board foot calculators on the internet or an app for your phone in your App store.

You will find that the better quality the board the, higher the price. Some places are labeling some of their boards PRIME which are now going for a premium price.

If they let you search through a stack of lumber, you will probably find some very nice boards to choose from. If you only need small cuttings, then you can probably save some money by buying a lesser quality board, sometimes a knot can add a lot of character to a box.

Looking at some wood characteristics!

Ash - A wood similar to oak with a straight and regular grain pattern. You should look for boards that are mostly light to white in color as they contrast very well with a darker wood such as walnut. Ash is easy to work with and will accept glue readily. Works best with a natural stain, darker stains may blotch. Ash is usually an affordable wood.

American Elm - This wood is not used very often, but I find that when you find a nice board and contrast it with a dark piece of wenge, it make for an outstanding box. Look for boards that are uniformly brown in color with a nice grain pattern on it. Can be fuzzy after planning, but sands easily. It reacts well to gluing and staining. Elm is generally moderately priced.

Black Cherry - A long time favorite of woodworkers. A little pinkish to reddish brown when fresh cut, but will darken with age when exposed to light. You do need to use a cherry stain to bring out that rich color of the wood. It is a very stable, straight grained wood which machines and sand easily having a very pleasant odor. Cherry does tend to be a bit pricier than some other woods.

Black Walnut - Another long time favorite of woodworkers. The best walnut is uniform in color that looks pale brown/gray to a dark chocolate brown/gray. It is getting harder to find good walnut without a lot of sapwood, so you may need to sort through some boards. It machines and sands easily. Using a natural or a light walnut stain will bring out the color of the wood. Walnut tends to be one of the pricier domestic hardwoods and can often garner a premium price.

Maple - The best boards are nearly white in color. Fairly easy to work with but can be brittle and burn when using a router. Works best when using a clear finish, stains tend to blotch and will need a pre-conditioner. Maple works well as an accent piece. Other maple varieties such as Bird's Eye Maple and Curly Maple can be strikingly beautiful when finished. Maple is usually moderately priced.

White Oak - A strong and beautiful wood, much heavier than many of the other domestic hardwoods. Can be nearly white to a light brown tone. It's grain is usually straight but can be coarse. Quartersawn boards tend to have prominent ray fleck patterns. It does work well with machines, glues well and accepts stain. Some people like to avoid oak or other large pored woods as the flock lining sometimes may bleed through the pores, however that can be avoided with proper surface preparation which will be covered in the finishing chapter. White oak may cost a little more than red oak, but is still an affordable wood.

Don't limit yourself to these types of wood. See what regional varieties you have available. Do try something different if it is available. You may be rewarded with something truly unique.

Exotic woods from around the world play a large part in making your band saw boxes stand out from other boxes. They can add color to a box like no other wood can. However, some of the more vibrant ones do tend to darken over time when exposed to sunlight. You may be able to slow down the darkening process depending on the finish that you use. These are some of my favorites.

Bloodwood - A tropical South American wood. You should look for boards that are bright to vivid red. It can be found in some extremely wide boards. It is very dense and does dull the tools. You do have to blow off the sanding residue which may tint adjoining pieces. A clear to light stain really makes the color "pop-out" at you. Bloodwood can be expensive depending on where you buy it. Bloodwood will darken with age.

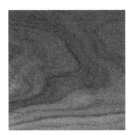

Padauk - A tropical African wood. An interesting reddish orange to a deep brownish red in color when first cut. It works much easier than bloodwood. Like bloodwood, you do have to blow off the sanding residue which may tint adjoining pieces. A clear to light stain will bring out it's natural color. Padauk is generally cheaper than bloodwood.

Purpleheart - Mainly comes from Central and South America. Look for boards that favor the more purplish color over the ones that are brown toned. It is a fairly dense wood that will easily burn when being routed, cut or sanded. Using a natural stain is best to bring out that purple color that you desire. It does darken with age and when exposed to UV light. Works well on band saw boxes as an accent and not the main focal point. Purpleheart is abundantly available and fairly moderately priced.

Sapele - A tropical African mahogany substitute that I like much better. Usually a uniformly brown to reddish brown in color, comes either flat sawn, rift sawn or quarter sawn (ribbon pattern) will give you a shimmery effect depending on how the light strikes it. Look for boards with a unique grain pattern. It is sometimes difficult to machine with some tearout possible, however I find that it does sand easily and looks great with a clear stain. Sapele is moderately priced and readily available.

Wenge - A tropical African wood. Tends to be a dark brown to blackish in color with light streaks in it's grain pattern. Will turn almost all black, except in some of the grain areas even with a clear stain applied. The grain can be wavy and difficult to get perfectly smooth. This wood looks great when contrasted with quarter sawn oak or a light piece of ash. *Just a note from experience: splinters from wenge are very sharp and can be painful. They can become infected if not removed.* Wenge can be expensive, often double the price of walnut.

Don't overlook veneers!

Dyed Veneers can add just that tiny bit of color you need when they are glued between your wood blanks. They also help break up the different wood grains that are next to each other. Most veneers will come in 1/32 inch thickness for a thin line accent, but you can find some at 1/16 inch or more for a thicker line.

Chapter 3-
Design Considerations

You have purchased that nice piece of oak, walnut or sapele and you are ready to get started. So what comes next?

You're thinking that all I've got to do is cut my board to size, glue them up into a block and start cutting. Well...that is mostly true.

What size of block for the box will I need? What kind of design will it have? How many drawers or sections will be in it? Answering these questions will get you started.

If you were given the choice between the two stacks of cut wood pieces below, which one would you choose for your box project?

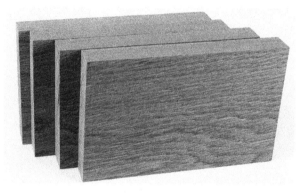

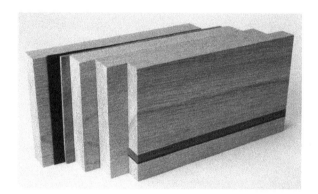

One made out of four pieces of solid oak or one made with four pieces of solid oak with the added color pieces. Boxes with color are more attractive. There are several ways that color can be added to a box. Adding a piece of exotic wood, colored veneer or a contrasting handle will do the job.

Many box books look for you to glue up uniformly thick pieces of wood, but I've learned that isn't always what gives you the best looking box. Since you are starting from scratch you can mix and match your woods to what you think looks aesthetically pleasing to you.

It is like making a sandwich at times. You have your outer pieces which are the same and then you fill it with what you like.

You also can mix different thicknesses, separating them with a slice of veneer, a contrasting wood or a thin piece of colorful exotic wood which will give the box a distinctive look.

Here is an example with two pieces of 5/8 inch walnut, two pieces of 1 1/4 inch sapele and a piece of 1/16 inch black veneer.

Here are a couple of more examples ready for gluing.

A Look at Orientation

The above two examples will be cut with the end grain orientation being up. That works well when your have a decorative strip glued into the front piece of the box .

At the right is an walnut box with honey locust accents with the end grain up for orientation. Notice how the honey locust adds to the attractiveness of the box.

Over the years I've found that many of the larger boxes look better with the cut pieces stacked on top of each other with the end grain in the front. You get a widely more uniform and distinctive grain pattern at the top of the box which is what most people will see first when they look at it. Take a look at the box below.

Notice how the striking the grain pattern stands out being on top instead of being sandwiched somewhere in the middle of the block. A nice combination of ash layered between pieces of sapele.

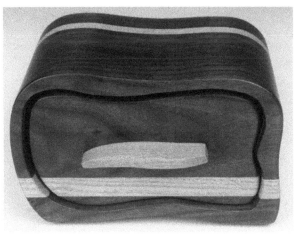

The larger blocks below will all be oriented with the grain at the top. You will see many of them in their finished state in later chapters.

Chapter 4-
Wood Preparation

There are still some prep steps to do before you are ready to create your band saw box after you have decided on the type of wood, size of box and pattern that you will be using.

In building your box, you will be gluing up several pieces of wood that are the same height and width, but not necessarily the same thickness.

If your boards are in the rough, then they will need to be planed...

...and edged.

Above prepared blocks ready for gluing

Some boards may need to be resawn into thinner pieces. The band saw is the ideal tool to accomplish this task.

Use a fence high enough to support your board. Feed at a steady rate.

Do a Google search or check out: https://www.highlandwoodworking.com/bandsaw-resawing-tips.html for additional band saw resawing safety measures and tips.

If you have ready made boards then you are all set to go.

21

Crosscut several varieties of 3/4" or thicker boards that you will be using into 18 to 24" pieces. You'll be able to get 2 to 4 boxes out of the pieces this long depending on the size of the box. They will also run through your planer better than shorter boards.

Rip several of them in half and a number of them in thirds (picture on the right).

Next add some color to the front piece of your box. These will mainly be used in the end grain on top boxes. I tend to glue up several of these pieces at one time so that I have them available for use.

Prepare a number of strips of thin slats of the various wood species that you will be using. Rip a variety of them in thicknesses from 1/8", 1/4", 3/8" and maybe some 1/2", also slice some dyed veneer if you have some from 18 to 24" in length.

Glue together and clamp according to your glue manufacturer's specifications. I usually leave them clamped up overnight.

Unclamp and scrape the dried glue off the boards with a chisel and then run them through your planer or drum sander to smooth them out. You may be able to flatten them with your portable belt sander with 80 to 100 grit paper. Be careful when sanding not to skew them.

These planed boards are ready for ripping and crosscutting to size.

Gather your pieces together. Select a contrasting, exotic wood or piece of veneer from your pile to pair with your wood pieces.

Sequence the pieces for the front and the back for grain up boxes; or one nice piece for the top of a stacked box as those parts will be the most visible.

This will be an end grain up box.

TIP - *For another look, cut freehand a gentle curve through your board and then glue in a piece of veneer instead of the solid slats.*

This will be a stacked box.

Spread plenty of glue on each block section making sure that there aren't any dry spots.

Determine the size and orientation of the box that you will be making, select the boards that you will be using, cross cut them to size a little wider than you need, then rip them a little wider to allow for final prep dimensions when you square up the box blank.

Clamp for several hours or over night.

The box blocks will look pretty messy after you remove the clamps.

The minimal amount of preparation you need to do is to scrape off as much glue squeeze out on the bottom of the box block, sand it smooth, then check that the box is square.

I prefer to work on cleanly prepared and squared blocks like the ones below rather than the ones to the center left. When you add your layout lines or your cutting pattern in the next step, they will be much easier to read. You will also know exactly how much box block you have to work with, and what the grain pattern will look like.

Squaring the Block!

There are a number of ways to square your block. One of the quickest ways is to use a joiner if you have one. Take off a small amount at a time to avoid excessive chipping. Join both the bottom and the top of the box. Make sure that the fence is square to the table.

Another way to square your box is to run your edges on a stationary belt sander with 80 to 100 grit paper (picture next page).

If you don't have a joiner or a stationary belt sander then all is not lost. You can also use a hand held belt sander on larger blocks or a palm sander on smaller blocks. It will take a little more effort, but you can get similar results. Keep a steady hand so that you don't skew the block. You should use either 80 or 100 grit paper.

To finish the squaring process, use a miter gauge and a wide blade to cut a little off of each end of the box. This cuts off the glue squeeze out from each end and allows you to see the block pattern better.

Check the block with a square for squareness, make corrections as necessary.

If the block is square then you are ready to move on to the next step.

OPTIONAL - Use a palm sander with 120 grit paper on it to clean up the block of any wayward pencil or tool marks.

Chapter 5- The Basic Traditional Band Saw Box

This chapter will be your reference guide to more complicated boxes found in the later chapters. I'll start with a few *small boxes* to give you the basics of making most of any kind of band saw box.

You've done all of the prep work. You've glued up your blocks, squared them off and now you are ready to start cutting. You will find that this part of making a band saw box actually goes the fastest. You'll be surprised as to how quickly your box takes shape.

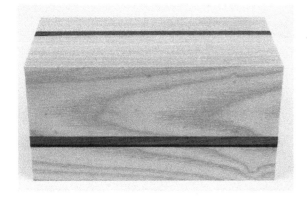

Block size is @6 1/2" in length x 3 3/8" high x 3" deep.

Before you begin, determine which sides of your block you want for the front and top. Take a few seconds now to mark them with a reference mark. I use a line or two across the top and right side of the box. I'll also use the letters **T** for top; **F** for front and **B** for back. I'll occasionally use an **arrow** to mark directionality for the front and back so that I always know which side is facing up.

Next you will need to decide what shape that you want the box to look like. I have several patterns that I've drawn and cut out of card stock that I use to trace the pattern on my block.

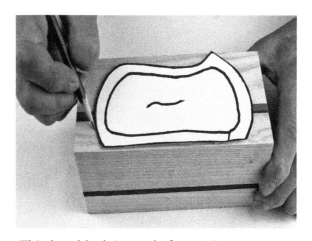

This box block is ready for cutting.

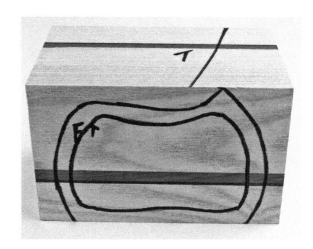

26

Alternatively, you can make copies of the pattern and glue them onto your block for cutting. *I do that when I have a particularly complicated design.* However, I prefer tracing the pattern, because I like being able to see the wood block as I am cutting it. The choice is yours.

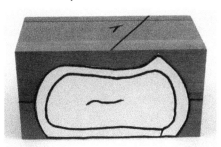

Glue stick glues work well for holding a pattern onto the wood block.

The Cutting Sequence - Bottom Cut

Step 1 - Set your fence so that is approximately 1/4" away from the blade.

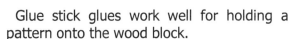

Make sure to square the fence to the table each time you reposition it.

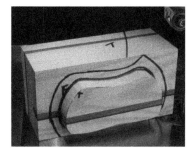

Step 2 - Cut off the back of the box using a push stick to guide your block along the fence. Use slow, even pressure as you don't want the back to bow away from the blade.

Step 3a - Remove your saw fence. You will be cutting out the drawer cavity first. Turn your box down with the pattern facing up. Start your cut from the bottom of the box following your pattern exiting back through where you began.

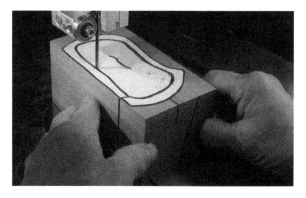

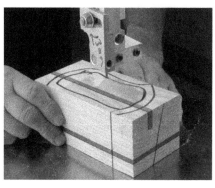

The entry cut for many traditional band saw boxes are made from the bottom or side of the block and left as part of the box design.

The Cutting Sequence -

Side Cut - an alternative method which will allow you to glue up the open saw cut.

Step 3b - This time we will start the cut from the side of the box. Follow your pattern around the drawer until cut free. Turn off your saw and then back out the blade. Use a small screwdriver to open a gap if needed.

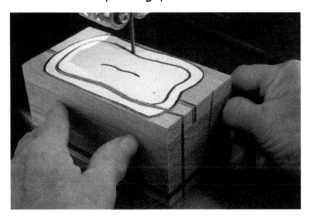

Step 4 - Glue and clamp the entry cut for at least an hour or two before you go on to the next step. A small screwdriver will help hold the cut open enough for you to apply the glue to the sides.

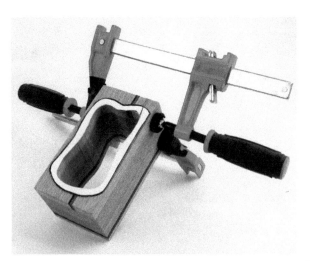

Wipe any excess glue from the inside of the box cavity now.

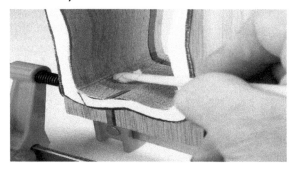

> **TIP** - Bamboo skewers wrapped with a little bit of paper towel make for a great tool to clean up the still damp glue. When the point gets dull, just sand it sharp again.

Step 5 - Before gluing the back piece back on, sand lightly the interior cavity of your box. Wrap some 150 grit paper around a dowel rod or thin stick and sand the interior cavity of the box followed with piece of 180 grit paper. *You are not trying to remove all of the saw cut marks, you are trying to take off some of the rough edges. Sanding too much will create a large gap when you put the drawer back in.*

An oscillating drum sander will also work.

Step 6 - Apply glue to the entire back of your box cavity. Use the reference marks that you made on your block to align it to the correct position. Clamp for at least an hour or more.

Note that the back on the side cut box will be skewed slightly due to the small amount of wood lost with the entry saw cut.

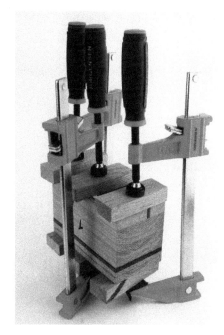

Let's start on the drawers next! Two examples

Make reference marks on the top and side of the drawer block, otherwise you may end up cutting the drawer upside down. Label front (F) and back (B).

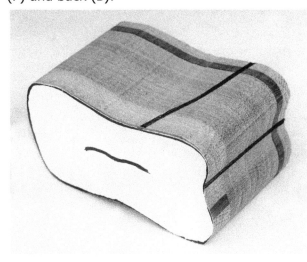

Step 7 - Set your fence so that is approximately 1/4" away from the blade. Make sure to square the fence to the table. Using a push stick, cut off the **back** of the drawer.

Step 8 - Readjust your fence so that it is at least 3/8" from the blade for a smaller box drawer. Using a push stick, cut off the **front** of the drawer.

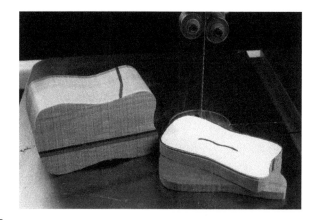

Step 9 - Place your back and front cut pieces into your box cavity then the block on top to level it with the box front. Using a square, mark your cut lines for the sides and bottom of the drawer (below and right pictures).

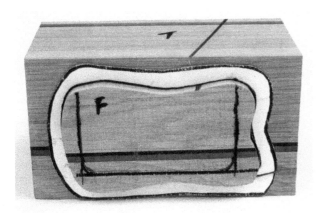

Don't limit yourself to one large cavity for your drawer. Put in more sections as space allows.

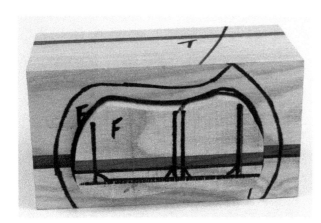

TIP - Draw a line across the top and the side of the cut out drawer and label back and front. *You will do this every time you cut out any section of your block.*

Step 10 - Remove the fence and cut out the inside of the drawer. Use a slow feed rate, staying as close to your lines as possible.

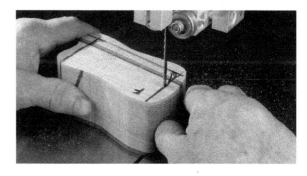

If your drawer has sections, cut off a small amount off of the top of the section. *This will allow for a neater finish appearance when you flock the drawers later.*

Smooth the edge by machine or hand.

Lightly sand the interior of the drawer if they are rough. However, in most cases that won't be necessary, if you will be using a spray in flocking liner.

Step 11 - Glue the three drawer pieces back together and clamp. Use your reference marks to put the front and the back in their right places aligning them carefully (picture top right).

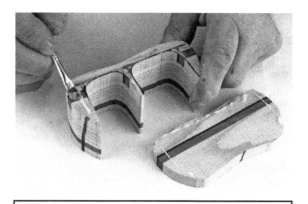

TIP - You can use a pin nailer filled with 23 gauge 1/2" pins to hold the back in place. (DON"T pin the front). These will help align the back and keep it from sliding when you clamp the parts together. *This will come in extremely handy when you work on some of the more complicated drawer glue ups that are in the later chapters.*

I often use scrap blocks as I'm clamping with my bar clamps. It helps to keep the pressure even around the drawer and helps to keep your pieces from bowing or breaking if you use too much pressure.

Step 12 - Cut out the outside form of the box. For most boxes this goes rather quickly and smoothly. Follow your lines as carefully as you can trying to maintain the same amount of distance as you cut around the edge of the box.

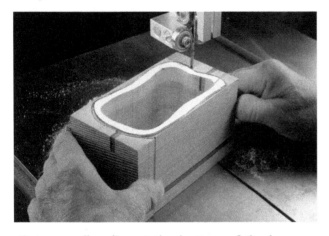

Cut a small radius at the bottom of the box so that it isn't entirely flat.

Your boxes (pictured below and top right) are ready for sanding which will be covered along with making handles and finishing in later chapters.

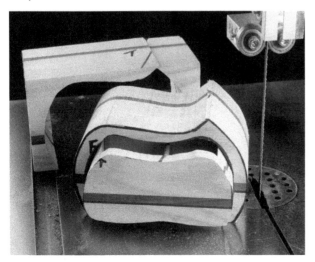

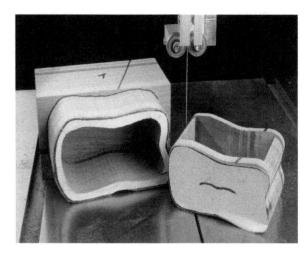

Options - To change up the look of your box, change the front panel of the drawer. Use your front cut off piece as a template to draw a new front on a contrasting piece of wood. Cut carefully then glue your drawer pieces together.

32

Chapter 6- Adding Trays, And Hidden Mini-Drawers

People like surprises, don't you? You don't have to limit yourself to large cavities and a few cut out sections in your band saw boxes.

Adding pull-out trays, hidden side or back mini-drawers that slide out adds a lot of individuality to your band saw box. The box also become more versatile as more pieces of small jewelry, that special coin or that extra folded up hundred dollar bill can be hidden away from sight.

Block size is @6 .0" in length x 3 3/8 " high x 3 1/2" deep.

Adding Pull Out Trays

A pull out tray will hide a "cubby hole" at the bottom of the drawer making for a nice hiding spot. *The tray needs to have a center support to be used as a handle in pulling it out of the drawer.* This will divide the tray into two sections.

Finished box *height* should be a minimum of 3 1/2 inches to 4 inches tall to allow for a main drawer of approximately 2 3/4 to 3 inches in height. This will allow for the tray/mini-drawer to be at least 1 inch or more in height.

A *length* of 6 inches works well. Box *depth* can also vary from a minimum of 3 1/2 inches to 4 inches for a simple box.

Step 1 - Follow **Steps 1- 6** from **Chapter 5** in cutting out, sanding and gluing the box.

Step 7 - Follow **Steps 7 and 8** in cutting your drawer front and back.

Step 9 - Insert the pieces into your box cavity. Use your square to draw out the pattern for your tray and bottom "cubby".

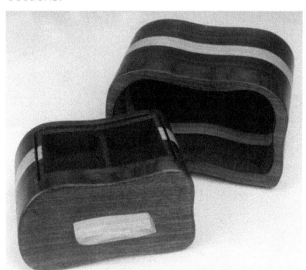

Step 10 - Cut the tray part out of the drawer block first. Then cut out the bottom part (below) of the main drawer. Make sure that you leave a lip for the tray to sit on when it is put back in.

Step 11 - Use lines to mark the top and end of your tray block like you did with your drawers. Set your fence at a little less than 1/4" away from the blade so that the sides will be @3/16" when sanded. Cut off the two sides.

Step 12 - Draw your pattern for the two sections on your try block and cut those out. *Remember the tray needs to have a center support to be used as a handle in pulling it out of the drawer.*

Step 13 - Sand all of the interiors lightly.

Step 14 - Carefully line up the three pieces of your main drawer, glue and clamp those parts together. Glue up and clamp the three pieces for your tray, glue and clamp the back on the box.

Step 15 - Go back to your band saw and cut out the box profile. Your box, drawer and tray are now ready for sanding.

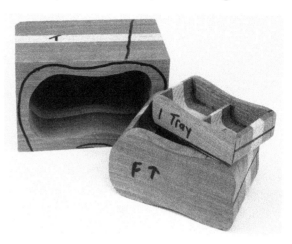

Adding a Side Mini-drawer/Tray

I call this a side door box because it has a small mini-drawer or tray that slides out of the side of the box when you tip it. The tray can have just one open section or can be divided into smaller sections. It just depends on your preferences. I find that having a tray height of 1 to 1 1/2 inches works well for most drawers.

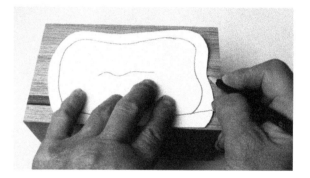

Step 1 - Draw your pattern. Follow **Steps 1- 6** from **Chapter 5** in cutting out, sanding and gluing the box.

Step 7 - Follow **Steps 7 and 8** in cutting your drawer front and back.

Step 9 - Insert the pieces into your box cavity. **Use your square** (picture next page) to draw out the pattern for the upper sections and the lower side drawer.

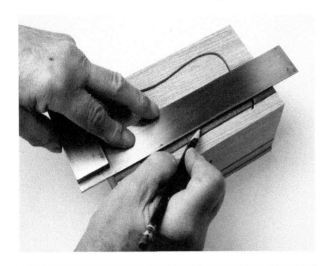

Turn the slat on it's side and draw the middle support section.

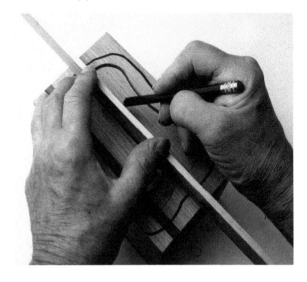

TIP - Cut and mark several 3/16" to 1/4" thick slats with various widths. When drawing out your patterns, choose how large of a mini-drawer (SD) you have room for, lay your slat on your block, eye-ball your line and draw the top and bottom lines at the same time (below).

Drawn pattern ready for cutting.

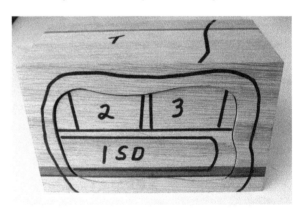

Step 10 - Cut the bottom mini-drawer part out of the drawer block first. Cut slowly to keep your cut as straight as possible.

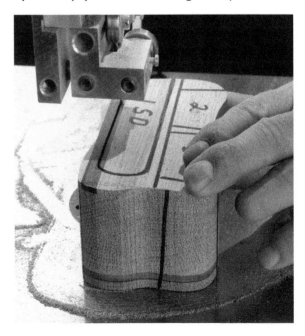

Then cut out the top sections of the drawer.

Parts are now cut out.

Step 11 - Take your *mini-drawer block* and once again use lines to mark the top and end of your block like you did with your drawer.

Set the fence at 1/4" or a little less away from the blade. Now cut off the two sides of your mini-drawer just as you did with your main drawer. Cut both pieces the same size.

Step 12- Lay out the sections for the mini-drawer. Turn on it's side and cut out them out.

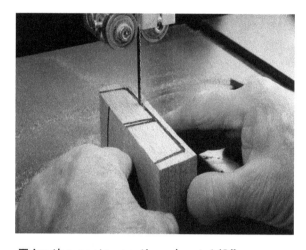

Trim the center section about 1/8".

Parts are ready for sanding, then gluing.

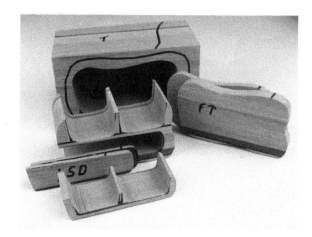

Step 13 - Sand all of the interiors lightly.

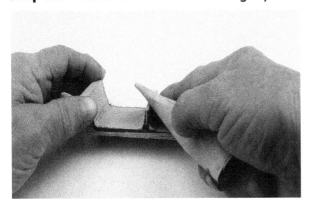

Line up the three pieces of your main drawer, glue and clamp those parts together.

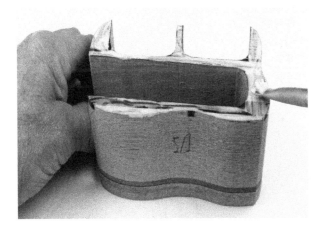

Line up your three pieces of your mini-drawer, glue and clamp them together.

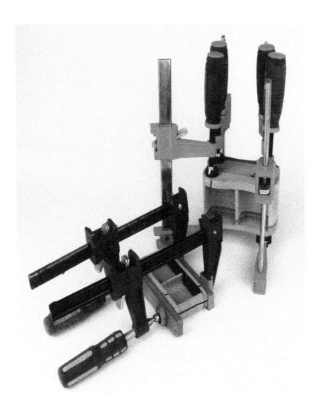

Step 14- Smooth out any glue squeeze out beads.

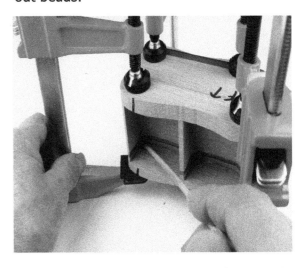

Step 15 - Go back to your band saw and cut out the box profile and small radius on the box bottom.

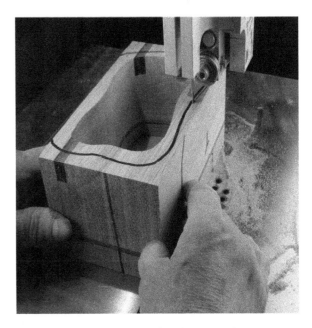

Your box , drawer and side mini-drawer are now ready for sanding.

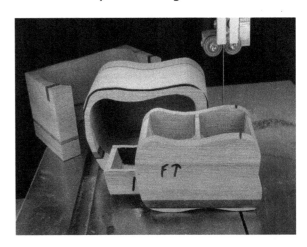

Adding a Hidden Back Side Mini-drawer/Tray

Adding a back side mini-drawer is a bit more complicated and has a different cutting procedure to follow than the pull-out tray or the side door mini-drawer. It will take you a little bit more time to complete.

Step 1 - Follow **Steps 1- 6** from **Chapter 5** in planning, laying out your pattern, and cutting out the drawer block.

Step 7 - The change here is that you will *be cutting off the front* of your drawer block first. Set your fence at 3/8" for the **front** of the drawer on a small box. *Do not cut the back side at this time.*

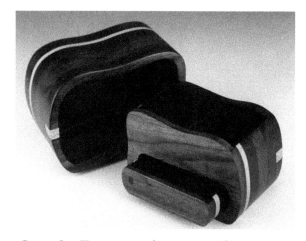

Step 8 - Insert the front cut off piece and the drawer block into your box cavity and draw out the pattern for the top section and back mini-drawer. Using the slats will make this easy.

NOTE that you will be having an entry cut that will be glued shut later.

Step 9 - Turn your drawer on it's side and slowly cut out the mini-drawer from the edge, back the blade out.

Do not cut out the upper sections at this time.

Step 10 - Glue the entry cut opening closed. Wipe any glue squeeze out in the mini-drawer opening at this time.

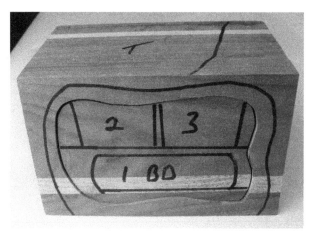

Clamp for an hour or longer. Take a coffee break.

Step 11 - Reset your fence on the saw to be @1/4" away from the blade and cut off the **back** of the drawer.

Step 12 - While the fence is still set at the 1/4" mark, cut the two sides of the back mini-drawer. *Make sure to mark your top and side reference lines first.*

Step 13 - Remove the band saw fence. Cut out the top sections of your drawer and the mini-back drawer section.

Lightly sand by machine...

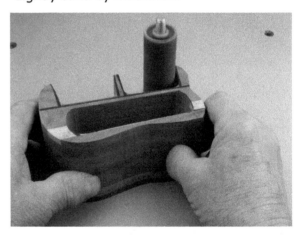

...or by hand.

Parts are now ready for gluing.

Step 14 - Glue and clamp the back of the box back on.

Glue and clamp the three parts of your mini-drawer back together.

Glue and clamp the three parts of your main drawer back together.

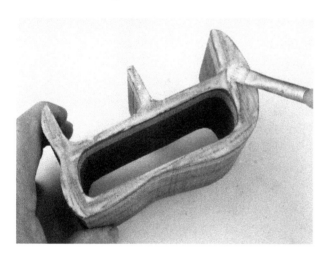

Using a 1/2" pin will help keep the parts from sliding.

Do not pin the front .

Keep clamped for an hour or more.

Step 15 - Go back to your band saw and cut out the box profile and small radius on the box bottom.

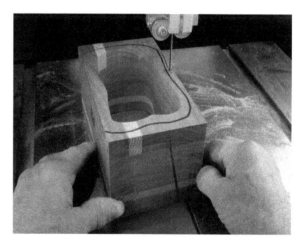

Your box, drawer and back mini-drawer are now ready for sanding.

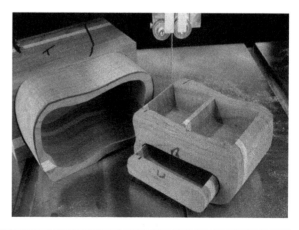

The more of these that you do, the easier it will be to do additional ones later. I've been making these for years and there are still times that I have to refresh my mind as to which step comes first and which step comes next.

Chapter 7- Basic Contemporary Band Saw Box

The contemporary band saw box has straight lines, a rectangular drawer and soft curves or gentle waves.

I've been asked many time. How did I get that perpendicular cut on the drawer cut outs without having a slight radius in them on your band saw?

In several of the following chapters I will be using the same techniques shown in this chapter to show you how that is accomplished. These steps in building the basic contemporary box will also be used to create even more complicated boxes.

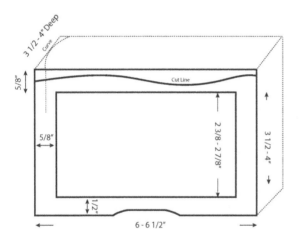

For a small basic contemporary box with a mini-drawer or a pull-out tray, a block size of 6 to 6 1/2 inches in length x 3 1/2 to 4 inches high x 3 1/2 to 4 inches deep works well.

My way may seem a bit complicated at first but it works well at keeping your cutting and gluing operations as simple as possible.

I won't be using a pattern with this box instead I will be using use a combination square to draw parallel lines across the two sides and the top and bottom of the block.

The **sides** are measured at 3/4" from each end. The **bottom** is measured at 1/2" for a smaller box and 5/8" for a larger box. The **top** line is measured at a minimum of 5/8" or a little more to give you room for your wave cut.

Basic box layout. Simply a rectangle within a rectangle.

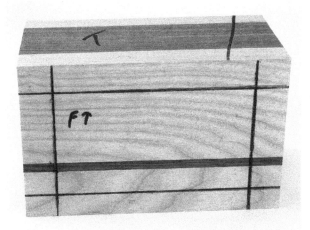

You will be using many of the same steps that you used in making the boxes in the last two chapters with a few changes.

Step 1 - Set your band saw fence approximately 1/4" away from the blade, check for squareness and then cut off the back of the box with the aid of a push stick.

Step 2 - Turn your box on to its back. Readjust your fence to line up with one of the drawer cutting lines. It doesn't matter if you start with the bottom line or the top. Now cut off either the entire bottom or top of the block.

Step 3 - Remove your fence. Using your miter gauge or do this freehand if you are steady, cut along your drawer lines but **STOP your cut** when you reach the opposite drawer line. Turn off your saw and back your blade out slowly (picture upper right).

Step 3 - (continued) Note that you will need to add a miter gauge extension to hold your block.

Move your block over and cut the other side drawer line the same way stopping when you reach the opposite drawer line.

Step 4 - At this point you are going to glue your bottom or top cut off piece back on. Only apply glue to the outer edges of your block up to the cut off line, line the two parts up and clamp.

Clamp for at least an hour or two before moving on to the next step.

Step 5 - Remove your clamps. Adjust the fence on your band saw to line up with the uncut line of your box and cut the opposite side. You should be able to tap out your drawer block now.

Occasionally you may have to finish cutting your side drawer cuts a little that you did in step 2 in order to tap out your drawer if your cut was off just a little.

TIP - This would be a good time to use your chisel and scrape any glue squeeze out that occurred with the prior clamping before gluing these pieces together.

Step 6 - Glue this piece on to your block making sure that you line up your two parts carefully.

Clamp for at least an hour. Wipe any glue squeeze out now while the glue is still tacky.

44

At this point I know that you are saying, **WHY** can't you rip the top and bottom off of the box block, then use your miter gauge to cut the two sides like the box below?

You can do that if you want and only clamp once instead of twice. HOWEVER, I've found that it is much easier and more accurate to line up and glue up only two pieces at a time instead of the four if you cut all your drawer lines at one time, especially when we get to more difficult boxes in later chapters. Your drawer will fit much better. The choice is yours.

Step 7 - Remove the clamps, sand the box interior with 150 grit sand paper followed by 180 grit to remove the rough edges.

Step 8 - Glue your back on now. Make sure to line up any decorative accent stripes.

Note - the back won't fit flush with the sides due to the slight amount of wood lost with your two saw cuts. Sometimes some of the accent stripes won't exactly line up. Get as close as a fit as you can when gluing.

Cutting out the box

There will be only a few minor changes when cutting out the form of this box. *You will be making four fairly easy cuts.*

Step 9 - Use your combination square to draw a line approximately 3/8" away from your drawer cut out on the front and back of the box on each side.

Use a French curve to make an arc to connect the two lines together on each side.

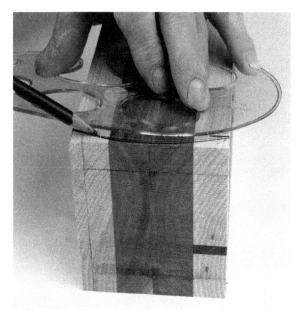

If you don't have a French Curve template, then use your own template cut out of cardboard that you've cut an arc on.

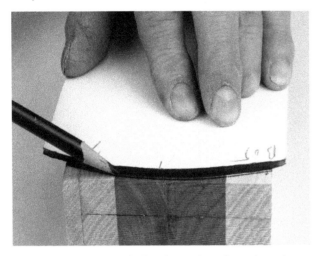

With the box on it's back, either free hand or with another shop made template, draw a gentle curve or wave across the top of the box.

TIP - Sand your bottom smooth before you move on to cutting out your box profile.

Cuts 1 & 2 - With the top up, follow your arc lines and cut off each side.

The two ends are shown cut off.

Cut 3 - Place the box on it's back, cut a small radius so that the bottom isn't entirely flat.

Cut 4 - Place the box on it's back. Beginning at one end of the box, cut a gentle wave across the top.

Completed rough cut box.

This box will have a side slide out mini-drawer and two upper sections.

> Your drawer block is going to have a very tight fit at this point and it may be difficult for you to slide it into your box cavity.
>
> Take a few minutes now, before you make any cuts on the block, to sand lightly the sides, most often the top and the bottom of the drawer block until it just slides into your drawer opening.
>
> *You will sand for final fit after the drawer parts have been cut and glued back together.*

There will be lots of drawer parts after your cutting is finished.

Sand the interiors lightly.

Dry assemble, then glue.

Clamp for at least one hour.

You can now proceed to lay out, cut and glue your drawer parts the same as you did in the last chapter with any trays or mini-drawers.

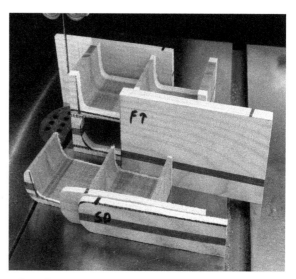

The box and drawer are now ready for sanding.

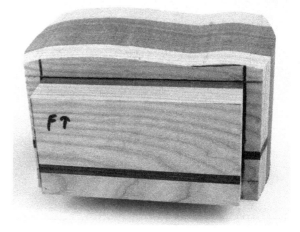

Adding a couple of more inches to the length of your box block will allow you to add an additional tray or mini-drawer.

Block size is @9.0" in length x 4.0" high x 3.5" deep

Lay out your drawer dimensions. Cut out the drawer block as shown earlier in the chapter.

Cut off the front and back of your drawer block if you want to have a mini-drawer on each side.

Draw out the sections for your drawer. *Cut out your sections and glue.*

Option - Cut off the *front* of the drawer only if you want a *back mini-drawer.*

Draw out the sections for your drawer.

Glue and clamp the opening for a back mini-drawer.

Set fence and cut off the **front** of the drawer block for a **back mini-drawer**.

Cut out the remaining drawer sections and the side mini-drawer.

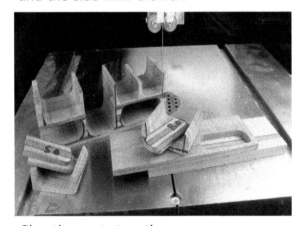

Glue the parts together.

Cut the box profile and you're ready for rough sanding.

So far we have covered the basics of making a band saw box along with adding some hidden drawers.

This chapter will take you through the process of dividing the drawer to add several more sections and additional hidden mini-drawers.

We are going to take the **basic one drawer contemporary box**, make it wider and longer, but not necessarily adding to the height.

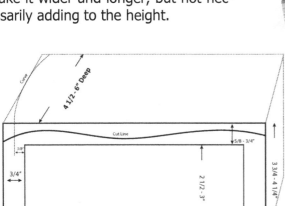

The **sides** are measured at 3/4" from each end to allow for a larger arc.

> The change from the earlier basic contemporary box is that your block should be at least 4 1/2 inches up to 6 inches wide (depth).
>
> The length can vary from 8 inches for a medium sized box up to 12 inches for a larger sized box. The longer the box, the more compartments you will be able to have.
>
> The minimum block height can be 3 3/4 inches. I prefer though that the block height be 4 to 4 1/2 inches tall, which will give a finished drawer height of approximately 3 inches for nicely sized compartments and mini-drawers. However, you can go a little less and have a slightly slimmer drawer.

The **bottom** is measured at 5/8" for a larger box. The **top** line is measured at a minimum of 5/8" or a little more to give you room for your wave cut.

Lay out your pattern as shown in **Chapter 7**. Remember to draw your orientation marks with a line or two on the top and side along with a **B** for the back, **F** for front and an optional **T** for top.

Step 1 - Follow **Steps 1 - 8** from **Chapter 7** for cutting out the drawer block and gluing the top, bottom and back together on the box block.

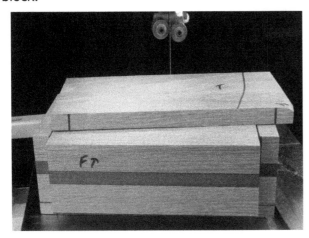

Step 9 - Your drawer will be tight, so sand just enough so that it fits into your box cavity.

Draw orientation marks on your drawer block (picture below) for the front, back, top and on one side of your block as shown in the earlier chapters. These will really come in handy when you reassemble your drawer.

Step 10 - Set your fence so that is approximately 1/4" or a little more away from the blade. Make sure to square the fence to the table. Using a push stick, cut off the *back* of the drawer.

Step 11 - Readjust your fence so that it is at least 1/2" away from the blade. Once again square the fence to the table. Using a push stick, cut off the *front* off of the drawer.

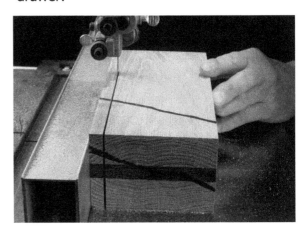

Step 12- Measure to the middle of your block, with a center or regular ruler, draw parallel marks 3/16 to 1/4" apart.

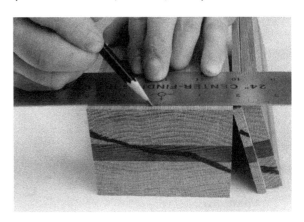

Step 13 - Set and square your fence to match one of your lines. Using a push stick, cut slowly to help maintain a straight cut.

Step 14 - Reset your fence to 3/16" to match your other line and cut that piece. *Use a support and push stick to keep your fingers safe.*

TIP - If you don't want to keep adjusting your fence then make a variety of shims matching the height of your fence of your most used widths. Place the shim along the fence and cut off your center piece (see picture above).

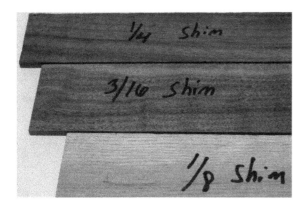

Step 15 - Draw out your layout diagram on your blocks. This drawer will have two side mini-drawers, one in front and one in the back, two deep sections and several smaller ones.

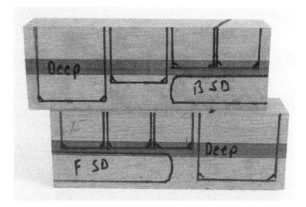

Step 16 - Remove your fence. Cut out your mini-drawers and other sections.

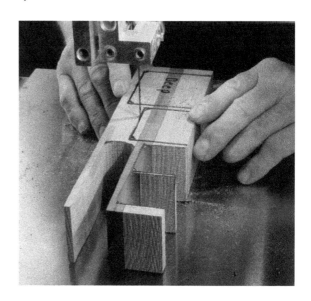

Step 17 - Mark the top and sides of any trays or mini-drawers. Cut the two sides off, then cut out the interior sections.

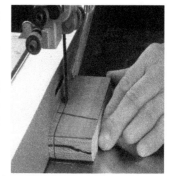

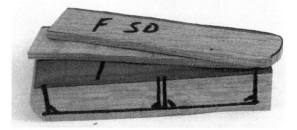

It is easy to get the middle and the back piece confused at times, so I use an **(M)** to mark the middle piece with the **(M)** facing the front of the box. Your fronts and back should have already been marked.

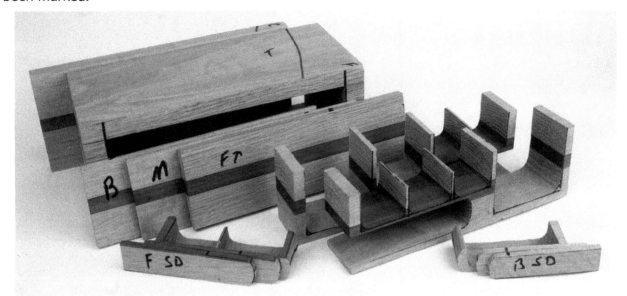

Step 18 - You will have a lot of parts. Collect and dry assemble them making sure that they are in the correct order, sand interiors.

Using the pin nailer here is extremely helpful since you will be trying to align 5 pieces without them sliding around when you glue them together. Line up and pin only the **back** *and the* **middle** *sectional dividers on their respective parts.*

Step 19- Glue and clamp your parts together trying to maintain as smooth of an assembly as possible.

Step 20 - Cut out the box profile as was shown in **Chapter 7.**

With the box upright, cut the two arc lines on the left and right.

Turn the box on it's back and cut a small radius on the bottom.

While the box is still on it's back cut a gentle wave across the top.

Your box is now ready for sanding.

Design Option I

You are starting basically with a block of wood for your box and drawer. There are many options available with that block for how you configure the sections.

This next option works well for people who need a larger cavity to hold a watch or a large necklace and it also incorporates two hidden side drawers.

Lay out the drawer pattern on your block as shown in **Chapter 7** to cut out the drawer.

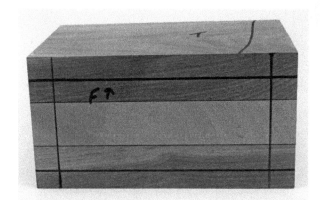

Step 1 - Follow **Steps 1 - 8** from **Chapter 7** for cutting out the drawer block and gluing the top, bottom and back together on the box block.

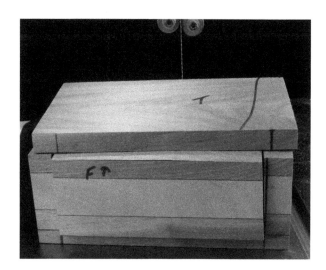

Step 9 - Set your fence so that is approximately 1/4" or a little more away from the blade. Make sure to square the fence to the table. Using a push stick, cut off the **back** of the drawer.

Reset your fence to 1/2" and cut off the front of the drawer.

We will be cutting your block in half again, but not quite yet. Let's add a large cavity and a hidden drawer first.

Step 10 - Draw out your pattern for a large cavity and any hidden drawers along with any other sections on the front of the block.

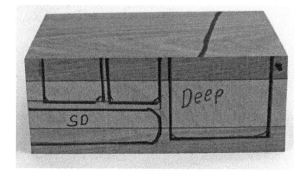

Step 11 - Only cut out the large deep cavity.

Step 12 - Measure to the middle of your block, with a ruler, draw parallel marks 3/16 to a 1/4" apart.

Step 13 - Set and square your fence to match one of your lines. Using a push stick, cut slowly to help maintain a straight cut.

Step 14 - Reset your fence 3/16" to match your other line and cut that piece.

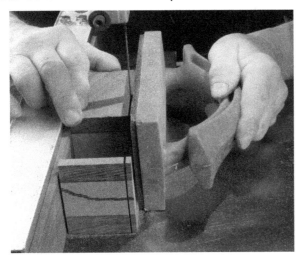

Step 15 - Draw out the layout diagram on the back block. This drawer will have two left side mini-drawers, one extra large deep section and several smaller ones.

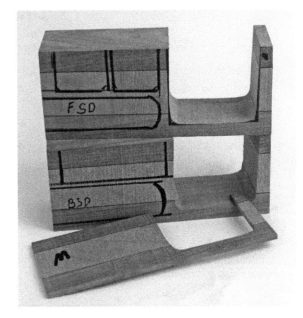

Step 16 - Remove your fence. Cut out your mini-drawers and other sections.

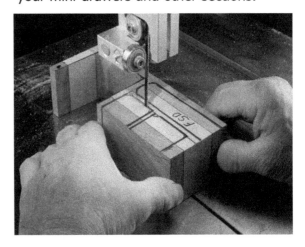

Step 17 - Mark the top and sides of any trays or mini-drawers. Cut the two sides off, then cut out the interior sections.

Collect your parts, dry assemble them making sure that they line up in the correct order.

Step 18 - Sand interiors if needed.

Glue and clamp your parts together.

Step 19 - Cut out the box profile as was shown in **Chapter 7.**

With the box upright, cut the two arc lines on the left and right.

Turn the box on it's back and cut a small radius on the bottom.

While the box is still on it's back cut a gentle wave across the top.

Your box is now ready for sanding.

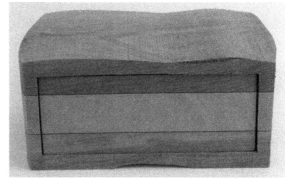

Design Option II

This next option is similar to option I except that the drawer will have a large pull out tray, a deep center section and a large side drawer that is not so mini.

Lay out the drawer pattern on your block as was shown in **Chapter 7** to cut out the drawer.

Step 1 - Follow **Steps 1 - 8** from **Chapter 7** for cutting out the drawer block and gluing the top, bottom and back of the box block.

Step 9 - Set your fence so that is approximately 1/4" or a little more away from the blade. Make sure to square the fence to the table. Using a push stick, cut off the **back** of the drawer.

Step 10 - Draw out your pattern for a large cavity and any hidden drawers along with any other sections on the front of the block.

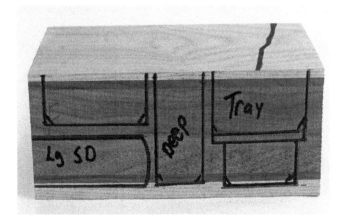

Step 11 - Cut out the deep center section, the tray and the large side drawer.

56

Step 12 - Measure to the middle of your block, with a ruler, draw parallel marks 3/16 to a 1/4" apart.

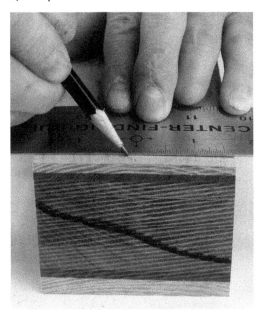

Step 13 - Set your fence to line up with one of the lines and cut slowly to help maintain a straight cut.

NOTE - the band saw blade will put a lot of downward pressure on to your block as you are cutting, insert a scrap block to reinforce the upper section of your drawer (see picture below).

Step 14 - Reset your fence 3/16" over to match your other line and cut that piece *(see parts in upper right)*.

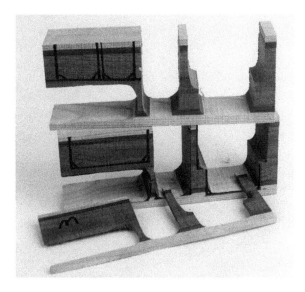

Now cut out the remaining sections.

Step 15 - *In order for your large side mini-drawer to fit, you will need to cut the sides a little heavier due to the corresponding loss of wood from the two center divider cuts that were made. After assembly, you will sand the sides of the drawer to fit the opening.*

Mark the top and sides of the large side drawer, cut the sides and then the middle section out.

The pull-out tray will need a special cutting so that it has a center divide that acts as a handle to pull it out.

Step 16 - Set your fence and cut the two sides like any other tray.

Mark the center and cut out a 3/16" middle piece.

Collect your parts, dry assemble them making sure that they line up in the correct order.

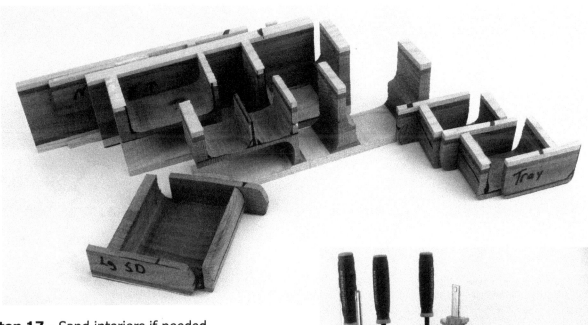

Step 17 - Sand interiors if needed.

Glue and clamp your parts together.

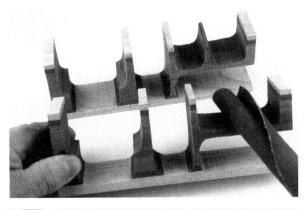

Step 18 - Cut out the box profile as was shown in **Chapter 7**.

With the box upright, cut the two arc lines on the left and right.

Turn the box on it's back and cut a small radius on the bottom.

While the box is still on it's back cut a gentle wave across the top.

Your box is now ready for sanding.

Design Option III

This next option will have a large side drawer along with a deep center section and two mini-drawers on the opposite side.

Lay out your drawer pattern as shown in **Chapter 7** to cut out your drawer.

Step 1 - Follow **Steps 1 - 8** from **Chapter 7** for cutting out the drawer block and gluing the top, bottom and back of the box block. back together.

Step 9 - Set your fence so that is approximately 1/4" or a little more away from the blade. Make sure to square the fence to the table. Using a push stick, cut off the **back** of the drawer.

Reset your fence to 1/2" and cut off the front of the drawer.

Step 10 - Draw out your pattern for a large cavity and any hidden drawers along with any other sections on the front of the block.

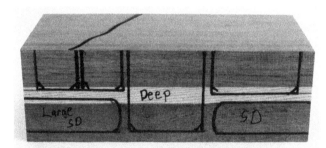

Step 11 - Cut out the deep center section.

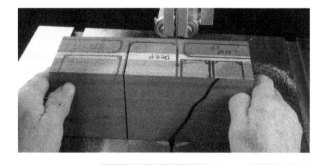

Cut out the large side min-drawer.

Step 12 - Measure to the middle of your block, with a ruler, draw parallel marks 3/16 to a 1/4" apart and cut on one of the lines.

Step 13 - Set your fence to line up with the other line and cut.

Cut out the middle divide.

Step 14 - Draw out your layout diagram on your back block. This drawer will have two left side mini-drawers, one large right side mini-drawer, one extra large deep center section and several upper smaller ones. *(layout has been drawn on the back side...will be flipped for gluing).*

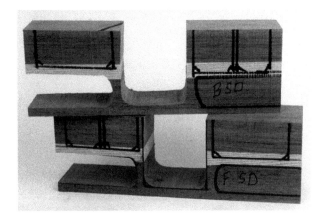

Step 15 - Remove your fence. Cut out the two remaining mini-drawers and the upper sections.

Mark the top and sides of any trays or mini-drawers. Cut the two sides off, then cut out the interior sections.

Remember to cut the large mini-drawer sides a little heavy for sanding after assembly.

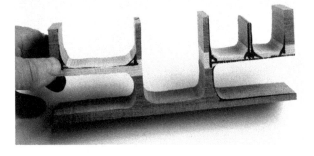

Collect your parts, dry assemble them making sure that they line up in the correct order *(picture upper right).*

Step 16 - Glue and clamp.

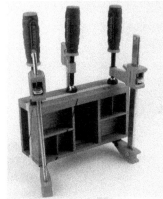

Step 17 - Cut out the box profile as was shown in **Chapter 7.**

With the box upright, cut the two arc lines on the left and right.

Turn the box on it's back and cut a small radius on the bottom.

While the box is still on it's back cut a gentle wave across the top.

Your box is now ready for sanding.

Design Option IV- Adding a Back Mini-Drawer

Adding a back mini-drawer or two to a split main drawer can be done following most of the steps that we did earlier in **Chapter 6.**

The cutting sequence will be a little different to reflect that we have a large split main drawer.

Let's prep the block for your back mini-drawer.

Step 1 - Follow **Steps 1 - 8** from **Chapter 7** for cutting out the drawer block and gluing the top, bottom and back of the box block. back together.

Step 9 - Set your fence at 1/2" and cut off **ONLY the front** of your drawer block, *do not cut* the back just yet.

Step 10 - Measure to the middle of your block, with a ruler, draw parallel marks 3/16 to a 1/4" apart.

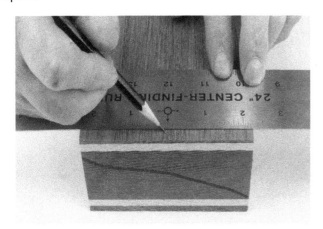

Step 11 - Set your fence to line up with one of the lines and cut.

Adjust your fence 3/16" or use your shim and cut the out the middle divider piece.

Step 12 - Draw your patterns on the two pieces. The front section will have a mini-side drawer. The back section will have a pull-out tray and one mini-back drawer.

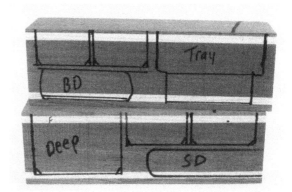

61

Step 13 - Remove your fence and *ONLY* cut out the back-mini-drawer or two depending on how many you want. *Do not cut the other sections at this time.*

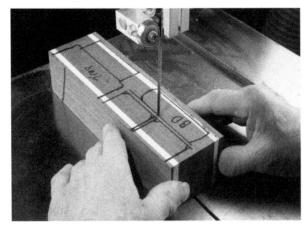

Glue the saw blade entrance way shut.

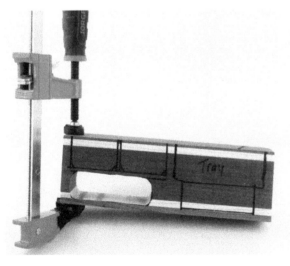

Step 14 - Reset your fence for 1/4" and cut the back off of your glued block (picture upper right).

Step 15 - Cut our the remaining sections for your drawer, pull-out tray and mini-drawers.

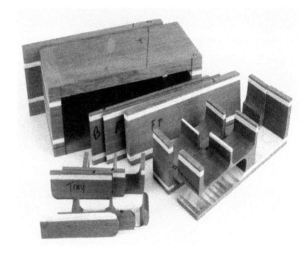

Step 16 - Dry assemble, sand interiors, then glue your parts together.

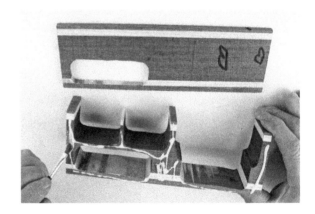

Step 17 - Cut out the box profile as was shown in **Chapter 7** and your box and drawer will be ready for sanding.

You aren't limited to these options. There are countless number of configurations using your drawer block. Add larger sections, make more smaller sections., change the sizes of the mini-drawers. It's your choice as to what the final drawer will look like.

Chapter 9- Larger Box Designs

In this chapter we are going to take a look at expanding the basic contemporary box into additional design possibilities. You already know how to make a variety of drawers, so we will be looking at a few variations of the box itself.

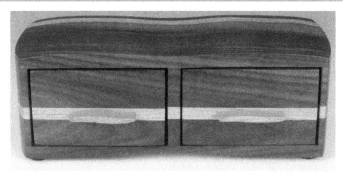

Side by Side Drawers

Think of this design as having two boxes made into one. Each drawer can house a different configuration.

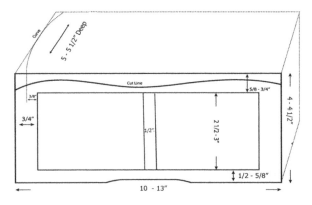

Step 1 - Draw a line for each side at 3/4".

Find the center and draw parallel lines 1/2" apart.

Draw a line for the top and the bottom at 5/8".

Finished diagram.

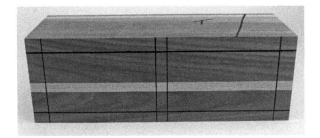

Step 2 - Set your band saw fence at 1/4" and cut the back off.

Step 3 - Reset your fence to 5/8" and cut off the bottom of your block along one of the drawn lines.

Step 4- Turn your block on it's back and cut each vertical line perpendicular **ONLY** until it reaches the horizontal crossing line at the top.

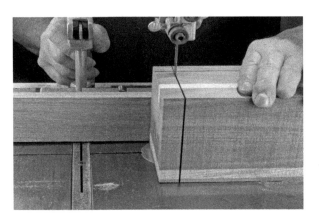

Carefully back your blade out of your saw cut each time, turn off your saw if necessary to do this.

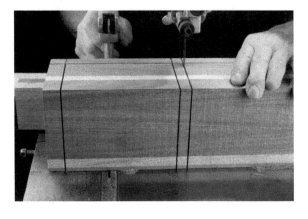

Step 5 - Line up, glue and clamp the previously cut bottom piece back on your drawer block.

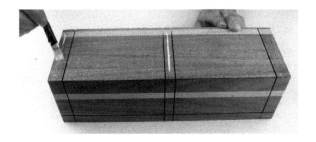

Step 6 - After an hour or two. Go back to your bandsaw and cut off the top of your box on your horizontal line.

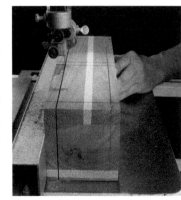

You should be able to knock out your drawers.

Use your chisel to scrape out any dried glue along the inside edge at this time.

Step 7 - Glue the top piece back on. Wipe any glue squeeze along the inside seam now.

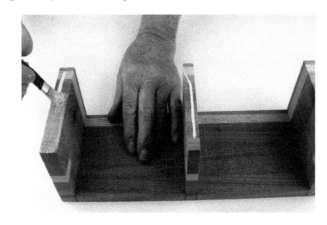

Clamp for an hour or two.

Step 8 - *Prepare your drawers. Refer back to the earlier chapters as to how to cut out the drawer sections.*

Configuring each side a little different from the other will increase the versatility of the box. Your choice!

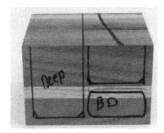 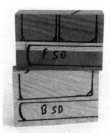

Step 9 - Sand lightly the inside box cavity and drawer parts.

Line up, glue and clamp the previously cut back piece of the box back on. The back won't be an exact fit due to the two saw cuts. Line up any decorative accent stripes as close as you can.

Glue the drawer parts together.

Step 10 - After an hour or two, remove your clamps and proceed to cut out the box profile as was shown in **Chapter 7.**

Starting by cutting an arc on each side of the box.

Place your box on it's back and cut a small radius curve under the bottom center of the box.

While your box is on it's back cut a gentle wave across the top of the box.

Your box is now ready for rough sanding.

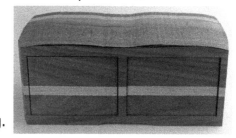

Two Drawers Small Bottom

I call this a Two Drawer Small Bottom box to differentiate it from the box with a large drawer on the bottom.

This box features two divided drawers that are approximately 1 1/4 to 1 5/8" deep with a number of sections in them. The sections can be configured many different ways depending on the sizes of items you want it to hold.

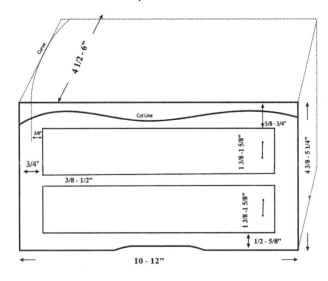

Step 1 - Draw a line for each side at 3/4".

A good size for this box is to have a block that is approximately 10 to 12 inches long by 4 1/2 to 6 inches wide by 4 3/8 to 5 1/4 inches in height. The measurements can vary depending if the drawer is divided or not.

Step 2 - Find the center then mark parallel lines 3/8 to 1/2" apart.

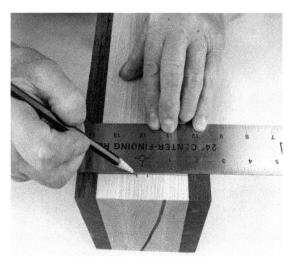

Draw a line for the bottom at 1/2 to 5/8".

Draw a line at the top at 5/8 to 3/4".

Draw your parallel lines.

66

Step 3 - Number the horizontal lines 1 - 4.

Step 4 - Set fence at 1/4" from the blade and cut of the back of the box.

Step 5 - Place your box on it's back and set your fence to match **line 3.** Cut along that line keeping a straight cut all the way to the end.

Reset your fence and cut along **line 1** all the way to the end. Your box will be in two pieces.

Note - Cutting line 3 first, then line 1 allows you to have smooth contact along your fence.

Step 6 - Turn your block on it's back and using your miter gauge, cut each perpendicular vertical line **ONLY** until it reaches the horizontal crossing line at the top of each of your two box blocks.

Do that for all four lines *stopping* at the horizontal line.

Carefully back your saw blade out of your saw cut each time, turn off your saw if necessary to do this.

Step 7 - Glue and clamp your parts back together.

After an hour or two you can remove your clamps and go on to the next two cuts.

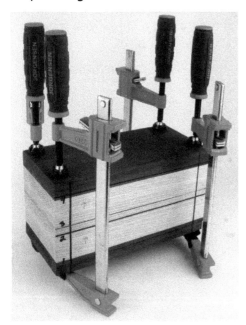

Step 8 - Place your box on it's back and set your fence to match **line 2**. Cut along that line.

Readjust your fence and cut along **line 4**.

You should be able to remove your two drawer blocks at this time.

NOTE - You could also cut **line 1** then **line 4** to get your two box pieces; or you can cut **line 2** then **line 3** for your two box pieces.

Scrape out any glue beads from the previous gluing before moving on to the next step.

Step 9 - Glue and clamp your parts back together. Scrape out any glue squeeze out now.

Step 10 - Remove the clamps after an hour or two. Sand lightly the inside drawer cavities.

Line up, glue and clamp the back on the box.

Step 11 - After an hour or two you can remove the clamps and proceed to cut out the box profile as was shown in **Chapter 7**.

Start by cutting the arc on each side of the box.

Place the box on it's back and cut a small radius curve under the bottom drawer cavity.

While the box is on it's back, turn it towards the top and cut a gentle wave across the top of the it.

Your box is now ready for rough sanding.

Making the Drawers - Make a straight divide or go curvy!

Step 12 - Set your fence for 1/4" and cut off the backs of each drawer.

Step 13 - Mark the center and offset 3/16" towards the back side of the drawer.

Step 14 - Use a shop made curved template to draw your drawer front profile and middle divider profile along the two marked lines.

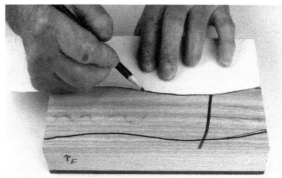

The drawer lay out.

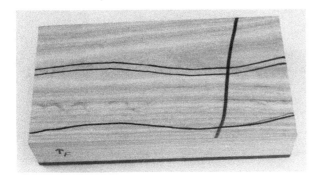

Step 16 - Draw out your drawer patterns on each block.

Step 15 - Free hand cut the curves.

Step 17 - Cut out the drawer sections.

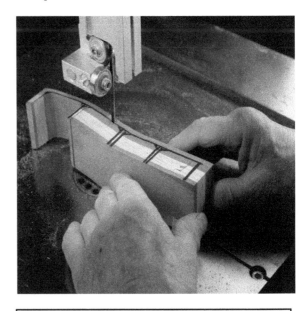

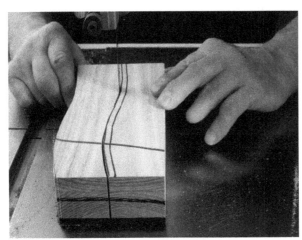

TIP - For safety it is best to tape a shim on to your drawer block to keep it level for cutting and keeping the insides squared up.

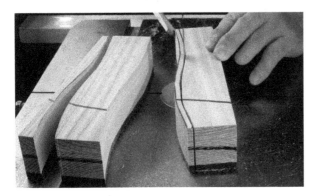

70

Step 18 - Trim 1/8" off the middle dividers.

Step 19 - Round over the dividers and sand lightly.

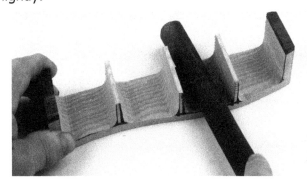

Step 20 - Line up your pieces for assembly.

Apply glue.

A 1/2" pin on the **back and middle pieces only** will help hold the parts together during gluing.

Clamp for an hour or more.

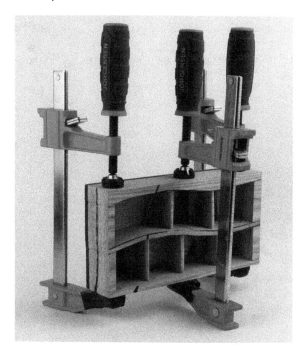

Insert the drawers into your completed box and check for fit. Both are ready for sanding.

71

Two Drawers Large Bottom

The box features a similar sized top drawer as the earlier Two Drawer Small Bottom box, but now has a larger sized bottom drawer which is why it is called a large bottom box.

This box size will accompany a pull-out tray, or a number of hidden side or back drawers. As in the previous box, the sections can be configured many different ways depending on the sizes of jewelry or keepsake items you want it to hold.

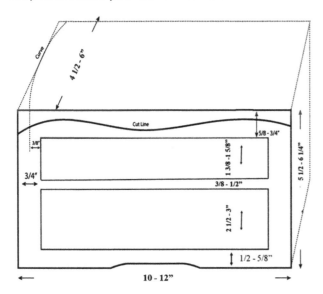

Step 1 - Draw your lay out lines according to the diagram below. Label the horizontal lines 1-4.

The vertical lines from each side are 3/4" from the edge of the box.

The bottom horizontal line is at 1/2". The top horizontal line is at 5/8".

Draw your two middle lines 3/8-1/2" apart so that your bottom drawer is at least 2 3/4 to 3" in height. The top drawer should be at least 1 1/4" in height.

A good size for this box is to have a block that is approximately 10 to 12 inches long by 4 1/2 to 6 wide by 5 1/2 to 6 1/4 inches in height. The measurements can vary depending if the drawer is divided or not.

Steps 2 - 11 - Follow the same cutting, gluing and clamping sequence of steps that were used in making the **Two Drawer Small Bottom** box earlier in this chapter.

Make the Drawers

Step 12 - Prepare your drawers blocks as shown in earlier chapters.

*Refer back to **Chapter 8** for the cutting sequence to make divided drawers especially if you plan to have a slide out back mini-drawer or two as the cutting sequence is different than the usual drawer cutting sequence.*

The drawers in this box are best suited to have straight cuts since the large bottom drawer will have a hidden mini-drawer or a pull-out tray. Curved drawers can be made, but they will take more planning and special cutting. That is something you can experiment with.

Chapter 10- Going Multi-Dimensional

The Contemporary Box designs so far have featured a flat front and back with an arc for the sides and a wavy top.

Let's go a step further and make these boxes more multi-dimensional by adding a gently curved front or a gently curved front and back.

The mid-sized to larger one drawer boxes or the larger two drawer boxes work out the best for the added dimensions. However, even a curve on a smaller box will work too.

The majority of the steps are the same as making a basic box.

Choose your box size, it can be a mid-size to large one drawer large bottom or a Two Drawer Small or Large Bottom box.

*You will need to **increase the width** of your block at least 1/2" to accommodate the curve on the front of the box or 1" for a curved front and back while maintaining the same sized drawers that we worked with in the earlier chapters.*

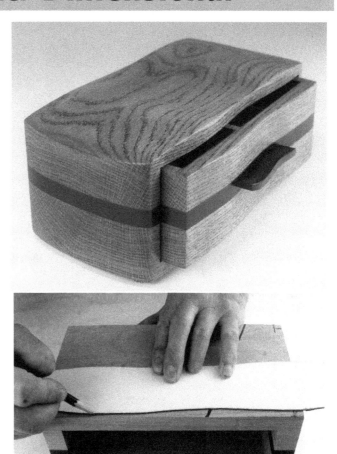

Planning the Drawer

To create a curved front on the drawers to match the curved profile of the box, you will need to make your drawer **front depth wider** than what was used in making your basic drawers.

Plan to **increase the depth of the drawer front** to at least 5/8" instead of the 1/2" that was used for the basic drawers to allow for cutting the curve and leaving you enough stock for the front.

Curved Front Only

Step 1 - Prepare the box block, cut out the drawer block or blocks and build your drawers as was shown in the earlier chapters.

Step 2 - Use a shop made template, or draw free hand a gentle wave along the front edge of the box block (picture in next column).

Step 3 - You will be cutting the front drawer profile at the same time as you cut the box profile. Insert your drawer blank into the box cavity. **Use several pieces of tape to hold the drawer securely in the box.**

Step 4 - Cut an arc on each side of the box.

Cut a small radius curve under the bottom drawer cavity.

Turn the box back on it's base and cut a gentle curve through the box and the drawers at the same time.

You will be cutting the drawer front blind, so cut enough of a gentle curve without going too deep that you don't leave enough material for your drawer front.

Place the box back on it's back, turn it towards the top and cut a gentle wave across the top of the box to complete the box profile.

The chapter on sanding will address how to sand both the box and drawer to maintain their profile.

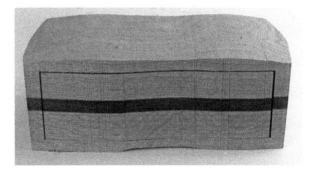

Curved Front and Back

This Contemporary Box design will complete the multi-dimensional approach by featuring not only a curved front, but also a curved back to give it a pleasingly beautiful profile.

Note: *In order for the box to have a curved back, the depth of the back cut will need to be increased from the standard 1/4" to 1/2" for a gentle wave or to 5/8" for a larger wave to accommodate the curved profile.*

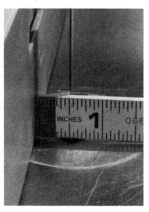

Step 3 - Use a shop made template, or draw free hand a gentle wave along the front...

... and back edges of the box block.

Step 1 - Prepare the box block, cut out the drawer block or blocks.

Step 2 - Prepare and complete your drawers as shown in earlier chapters.

You will also need to have the added depth for the drawers mentioned on an earlier page to allow for the curved front.

If you have a narrower box then you should make a non-divided drawer; If you have a wider box than you can make the divided drawers.

Before cutting your drawer blank you will need to decide if it is to have any pull-out trays, side or back mini-drawers.

Refer back to **Chapter 8** for the cutting sequence to make divided drawers especially if you plan to have back mini-drawers.

The cutting sequence is different than the usual drawer cutting sequence.

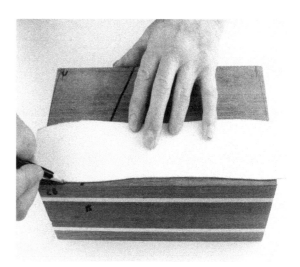

Step 4 - Use several pieces of tape to hold the drawer securely into the box going all the way over the back side of the block.

Step 5 - Complete the cutting sequence. Cut the bottom radius.

Cut the arc on each side.

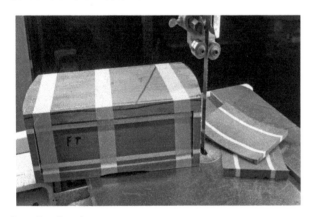

Cut the back wave cut.

Cut the front wave.

Place the box back on it's back, turn it towards the top and cut a gentle wave across the top of the box to complete the box profile.

The completed box is ready for sanding.

Two Drawer Boxes

Follow the same procedures as the previous boxes to have a multi-dimensional large box.

Draw a wave across the front and back edges.

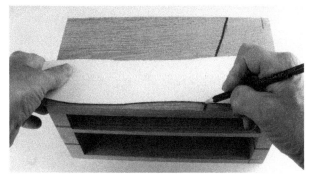

Tape the drawers inside the box cavities.

Cut the bottom radius.

Cut the arc on each side.

Cut the back wave.

Cut the front wave.

Cut the top wave.

Ready for sanding.

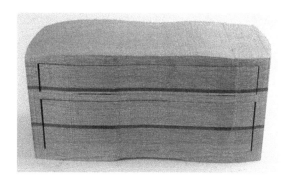

Take the design a step further ...

...by adding curves to the top and bottom of the drawer which will really make your mid to large one drawer or two drawer side by side box stand out.

Steps 1 - 3 - Follow the basic steps in making a curved front and back box.

Draw your lay out lines for the size of your drawer that you will have with curved lines at the top and the bottom of the drawer

Set your fence for 1/2 to 5/8" away from the blade.

Cut off the back of the box.

Steps 4 - 9 -Turn your box on it's side and cut free hand either the top or the bottom of the drawer.

Using your miter gauge cut the two vertical lines up to the opposite drawer line.

> **Optional -** *Instead of a straight cut, free hand a curved cut on the drawer sides up to the opposite drawer line.*

Glue and clamp together the cut off piece back on the box block as was shown to you in **Chapter 6** making the basic contemporary box.

After an hour or two, remove the clamps and now cut free hand the opposite wavy line to release your drawer.

Glue and clamp the top or bottom back on.

Step 10 - Prepare and complete your drawers as shown in earlier chapters.

If you have a narrow box then you should make a non-divided drawer; If you have a wider box than you can make the divided drawers.

Before cutting your drawer blank you will need to decide if it is to have any pull-out trays, only side slide out mini-drawers or back slide out mini -drawers.

Refer back to **Chapter 8** for the cutting sequence to make divided drawers especially if you plan to have slide out back mini-drawers.

The cutting sequence is different than the usual drawer cutting sequence.

> **Note -** *Your drawer blocks need to be completed before you proceed to cut the box profile below.*

Steps 11 - 16 - Insert the completed drawer block into the box cavity and tape the drawer to the box block.

Start by cutting the arc on each side of the box.

Turn the box towards the front, cut a gentle curve through the box and the drawers at the same time. ***See the previous page for details and pictures.***

Turn the box on it's base and cut the curve across the back.

Place your box is on it's back and cut a small radius curve under the bottom drawer cavity.

While your box is on it's back, turn it towards the top and cut a gentle wave across the top of the box.

Your box and drawers are now ready for rough sanding.

Pictured above is a side by side box with bottom and top curved drawers.

Chapter 11-
Tower Box

The Tower Box doesn't appear to be your typical band saw box. It has straight lines and angled drawers that could have been cut on the table saw.

A hidden back mini-drawer, a couple of side mini-drawers, large cavities and multiple sections with-in the drawer combinations contribute to the box's functionality and distinctive design.

The box style does create some unique challenges in the building process.

A number of the steps, but not all, will be shown again since many of the techniques used in making the box and drawers are the same ones that were used in the earlier chapters.

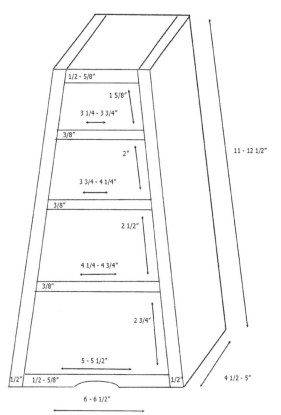

The block for this box will be large. This combination of walnut and sapele measures 12 1/2 inches high x 6 5/8 inches wide x 4 5/8 inches deep. Make sure that the block is square on all sides.

79

Draw a pattern to fit the block size that you have. Adjust the drawer sizes depending on the size of the block that is being used.

The drawer openings on this box are 5 1/4 x 2 3/4" being the largest, 4 5/8 x 2 5/8", 4 1/8 x 2 1/8" and 3 5/8 x 1 3/8"at the top. The sides are 1/2", the bottom is 5/8" with the top being 3/4". The separation between each drawer is 3/8". Change them to fit your needs.

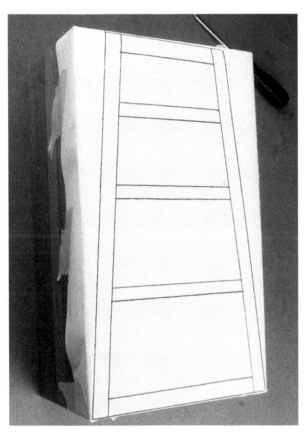

One way to draw out your pattern on the block is to use a punch awl to place a mark on the intersecting lines on one side.

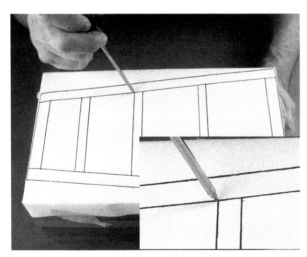

You could also use a ruler to mark the dimensions and then follow the layout steps in the next column.

It is not recommended that you cut on the paper pattern.

Remove the pattern and connect the dots or skip using the awl and use a ruler to draw the side lines and mark the measurements for each drawer and drawer separation.

Use a square from the side to draw your lines from each mark...

...or a combination square from the bottom.

Step 1 - Set the band saw fence 1/4" away from the blade, check for squareness and then cut off the back of the box. using a push stick.

Note - A taller shop made fence was clamped to the band saw table to guide the cut given the larger size of the box itself.

Step 2 - Turn the box on to its back. Slowly cut to just the outside of one of the side box lines.

Step 3 - Sand the cut off edge up to the drawn line (picture top right).

Step 4 - Set the fence to match the parallel inside line and cut.

Step 5 - Remove the fence. Cut along the drawer lines with the aid of a miter gauge. **STOP the cut** when you reach the opposite drawer line. Turn off the saw and back the blade out slowly.

A clamp will help hold and control the block for a straighter cut.

81

Step 6 - Apply glue to the outer edges of the block up to the cut off line, line the two parts up and clamp for an hour or two.

Step 7 - Remove the clamps and cut off the wedge on the opposite side and sand up to the drawn line. Set your fence and cut off the opposite side of the box.

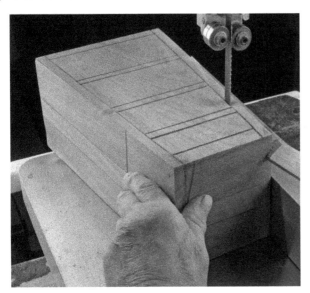

Step 8 - Apply glue, line up and clamp. A pin will help maintain the drawer squareness and keep the parts from sliding.

Tip - Use the cut off wedges when clamping to help maintain the squareness of the box.

Place the box on the cut off back piece and draw a line along the outside to mark the tapered section for cutting before gluing on the back.

Glue the back on.

82

Clamp.

The only cut to be made on this box is to cut a small radius on the base so that it isn't entirely flat. Then sand the sides flush.

Make the Drawers

Making the drawers for the tapered box are pretty much the same as for any of the other boxes.

The largest drawer at the bottom will have a back mini-drawer. Set the fence at 3/8" and cut off the **front** of the drawer block, *but not the back.*

Measure to the middle of the block with a ruler, draw parallel marks 3/16" apart.

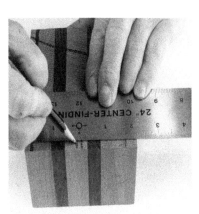

Set the fence so that you cut the center outside line towards the back of the drawer block.

Draw the patterns on each block. Cut out the back mini-drawer on the back block.

Glue the opening.

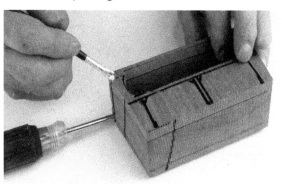

Clamp.

After an hour or two remove the clamps. Set the fence for 1/4" and cut off the back of the drawer.

Cut out the upper sections.

Divide the remaining drawers according to the directions in **Chapter 8.**

Draw out the sections on all of the drawer parts.

Dry assemble the drawer parts.

Glue.

Clamp.

Care has to be taken when sanding the drawer sides either by machine or by hand to maintain the right angle to fit the drawer back into the box cavity.

Setting up a jig on your sander helps to maintain that angle.

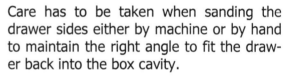

Insert the drawers, check for a uniform fit along the sides.

The box and drawers are ready for sanding.

Chapter 12- Sanding

If there is one part of any woodworking project that many woodworker's despise, it is probably sanding.

Sanding is dusty, gets everywhere and can be hard on your hands.

When sanding don't skip grits, work your way through from 120 to 150 to 180 or 220 grit. Complete sanding preparation usually leads to a good smooth finish on your project that people will admire and compliment you on for years to come.

Do I need lots of fancy equipment?

If you plan on making only an occasional band saw box for personal use or as gifts, then you don't need to have a lot sanding equipment. You can make the majority of the smaller boxes in this book by changing grits on a palm sander and following that up with lots of hand sanding. However, there are many kinds of power sanders out there that will make the job go much quicker and easier. **See Chapter 1 for suggestions.**

I usually break the sanding process down into two parts if I'm making a number of boxes at the same time. If not, then you can move from one step to the other.

The first step is rough sanding your box body and drawers. It is the initial step in removing saw cut marks, scratches, clamping and pencil marks. This step will also produce your final box profile. A majority of the rough sanding is best done using your power sanding equipment.

The second step is finish sanding where your box gets prepared for staining and then applying your finish. Initial finish sanding can be done by power equipment, *but the final sanding should always be completed by hand.*

Rough Sanding

A stationary belt sander makes quick work of sanding out saw marks and getting your box sides to uniform dimensions. Ninety percent of my rough sanding is done on the belt sander. They come in many different sizes.

The roller edge works well at smoothing out the curved edges. I generally use a 120 grit aluminum oxide belt to do the majority of the rough sanding.

85

A palm sander will work to complete the rough sanding, but it will take a lot more time.

Start with 100 or 120 grit then move up to 150 grit to erase the saw marks. You will need to sand enough of the sides to equalize your side wall dimensions.

A palm orbital sander works especially well on flat surfaces.

Another option is to use a large cylinder on an orbital drum sander.

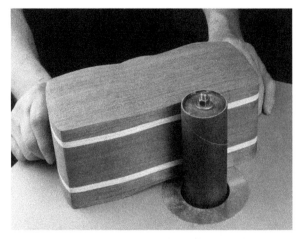

Large inflatable drum sanders are a luxury. They work particularly well with the finer grits. You can buy some smaller ones that will fit on your drill press, hand drill or lathe.

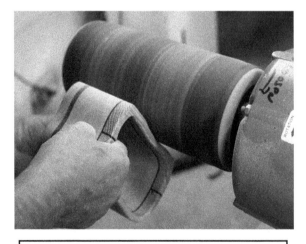

Tip - Which sand paper to use?

Aluminum oxide sand paper is heavier and will take more abuse for rough sanding. Switch to garnet sand paper for finish sanding by hand.

Rough sanding boxes with curved fronts and curved drawers requires a slightly different technique.

Put your drawer into your box cavity and rough sand them both at the same time which will maintain their profiles.

A belt sander will make the job go fairly quickly.

Using the palm sander will work, but will take more time to do.

Sanding Drawers

Sanding drawers takes a delicate touch. You don't want to over sand so that you have large gaps between your drawer and your box profile.

The same power equipment that are used for rough sanding can also be used efficiently for sanding the drawers.

Belt sanders are aggressive. Take only small amounts off at a time and check your results.

The versatile palm sander works well.

Moving on to Finish Sanding

Complete the final preparation with a thorough finish sanding.

Usually 180 grit paper will suffice for your final sanding if you will be using a film finish. Go up to 220 grit if you will be using an oil and wax finish.

You can use your hand held palm sanders efficiently to do some of the final sanding. However, the final sanding should always be done by hand. You have more control over your sanding and you can see areas where you need to sand a little bit more.

I prefer to soften the edges of the contemporary boxes with sandpaper.

You should have just a break in the sharpness of the edge that is smooth to the touch.

A sponge sanding block will roll over your routed edges. It also makes for a great support for your garnet paper.

Soften the inside edge too. A sponge sander works well here.

An option is to use your router with a 1/8 or 1/4" bearing round over bit to put a curved edge on your box body and drawer. I usually do this for my traditional boxes.

Using the router will create a uniform edge around your box. Practice on a few pieces of scrap wood to get the depth and look that you want.

Smooth out the edges.

A flap sander works especially well at smoothing out the curved parts of your boxes. It also does a quick job of softening the routed edges.

It does require a firm grip and a slow easing into the spinning wheel. I've had more than my share of boxes or drawers get pulled out of my hands.

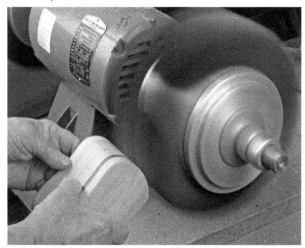

Run your fingers over your box, especially the edges to feel for rough or sharp areas and resand.

Cover thoroughly all sides of the box and drawers.

For a final check, hold your box up to a light and take a closer look for any wayward sanding scratches that you may have missed.

Once you are satisfied then you are ready to add a handle to your drawer and one step closer to finishing your project.

You may think that a handles only purpose is to pull the drawer open. While that is true, a nicely made handle can also be a decorative accent.

You've made this beautiful box, don't take the easy way out by buying a brass or wooden knob. They will not do your box justice as your own dimensional handle would be.

I've seen some great looking boxes at art shows over the years, but the handles on some of these boxes made it difficult to open the drawers. Some were too fat, some were not deep enough, others were too small.

A smooth to the touch handle makes the drawer a pleasure to open. A handle needs to be ergonomically sized so that it is easy to grab, wide enough so that your fingers can slide easily into it.

Handles should also be multi-dimensional. A smooth curve to the design is more attractive than a straight lined handle.

I'll have a few handle patterns at the end of this chapter.

You can make a handle in all kinds of shapes, sizes and dimensions. You can see from the examples above a myriad variety of handle possibilities.

An exotic wood handle made out of bloodwood, padauk, or wenge adds a touch of vibrant color. I usually choose an exotic wood to match any decorative accent striping that I had used in making my box.

Take a look at the handles on the drawers at the left, notice how the various woods compliment with the wood that the drawer is made out of.

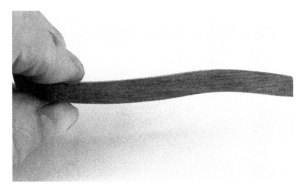

I prefer a longer handle. Finished handle depth should be a minimum of 1/2 to 3/4". Handle thickness can be as slim as 3/16" but 1/4" works well.

There will be some instances when a wider handle will be used based on the design of the box and drawer.

Making a handle takes only a few easy steps

Step 1 - Select the handle pattern that will go well with your box. Choose a piece of wood that will give you a little bit of room for cutting and sanding. Use the pattern to trace it on your wood piece.

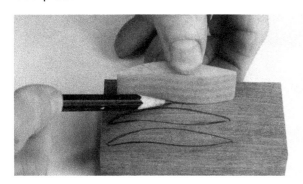
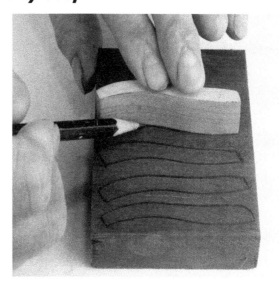

Step 2 - Cut slowly on your band saw. Use a push stick to keep your fingers away from the blade.

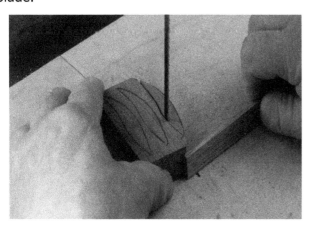

Step 3 - Sand the contours just enough to get out the saw marks. Don't forget to touch sand the ends.

It can be little tricky holding your handle on the belt sander with your fingers. Using a large spring clamp with the rubber ends removed works well.

The oscillating sander is a safer alternative or sand by hand.

Step 4 - Finish sand the top and bottom switching grits up to 180 grit paper. The edges will be sanded later after the handle has been applied to the drawer.

Step 5 - Use a small painter's brush to apply the glue. Use your finger to clear away glue too close to the edge.

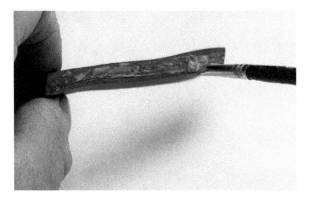

Step 6 - Hold your handle in place for a few seconds until it tacks up.

Slowly clamp your handle to your drawer so that it doesn't slide out of position. Keep it clamped for a half an hour or so to insure a strong bond.

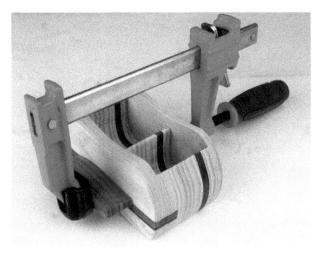

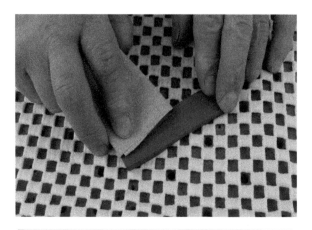

Tip - *Titebond No run No drip* glue is excellent for gluing on your handles. It is a little thicker than other glues, has good instant tact and as the label says, no run or drip.

Titebond Molding or Translucent glues are good alternatives.

Use a bamboo skewer to scrape off any tiny bits of glue squeeze out now while it is still tacky.

Step 7 - Add dimension to your handle by cutting a small arc along the front.

You can also use your belt or oscillating sander to sand the small arc along the front of the handle.

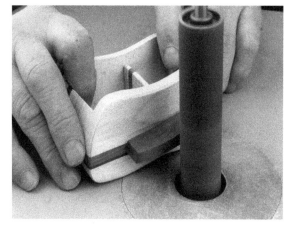

Step 8 - Hand sand the edges of the handle to take off the sharpness.

Follow that up with the sponge sander to further soften the edges and to clean up any random sanding or glue marks that were left over.

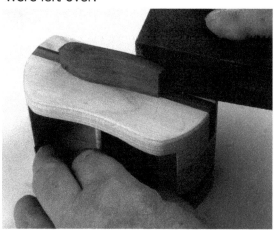

A curved drawer handle takes a few more steps to make

Making a handle for a curved drawer can be frustrating. I've cut and sanded what I thought was the perfect handle and spent a great deal of time having to tweak it to fit properly.

There is a little bit more prep work, but cutting, gluing, clamping and sanding the handle is mostly the same. Only a couple of additional steps are needed.

You will need to cut the handle to conform to the curve of the drawer as shown below.

Begin by following the steps in making the basic handle. Choose your pattern, draw it out, cut, and sand the top and bottom cut sides.

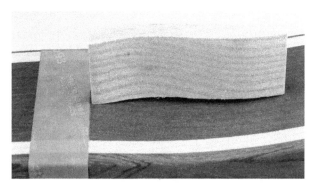
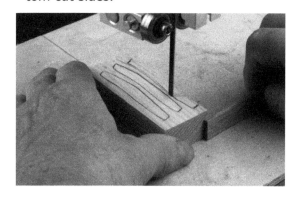

Step 1 - Mark a reference point on one side of the drawer front by placing a strip of tape where the handle's start line begins. Painter's tape works well and doesn't leave residue.

Step 2 - Use a contour gauge, if available, to form the shape of the drawer. Put painter's tape on your gauge also as a reference point.

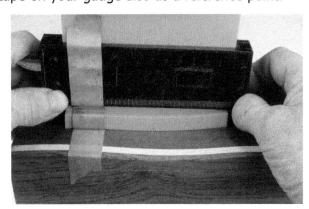

Step 3 - Place your contour gauge on your handle blank and trace the shape of the contour.

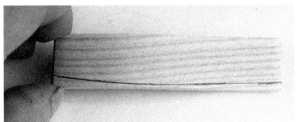

If you don't have a contour gauge, then place your box on top of the handle blank and use the bottom of the box to trace your form.

Step 4 - Carefully sand the edge of the handle up to the contour line you drew with the roller edge of your belt sander. *Note that I added a thin plywood base to close the gap between the belt and the sander table for safer sanding.*

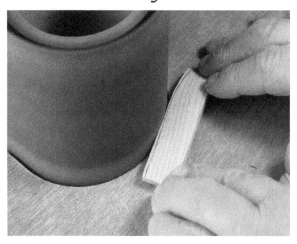

An oscillating sander will also work well.

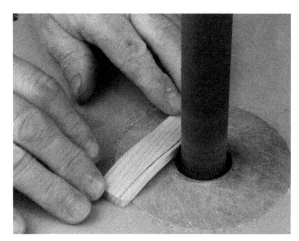

Here's the fun or frustrating part depending on how you look at it. Place your handle on the drawer and hold it up to a light to see if there are any gaps between the handle and the drawer body.

If there is a gap then you will need to tweak the edge with a few light swipes on sandpaper.

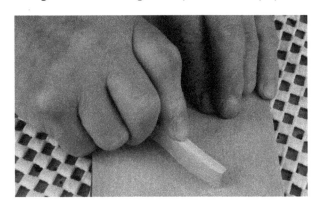

Recheck and tweak again until the handle fits snugly without gaps on your drawer body.

Sometimes it has taken me several tries to get a proper fit. Once you are satisfied then go on to the next step.

Step 5 - Check your fit, apply glue.

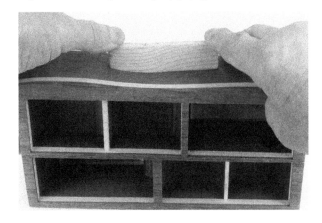

Keep clamped for half an hour.

Step 6 - Instead of an arc, sand the handle to mimic the contour of the drawer using whatever tool you have available.

Soften the edges as before.

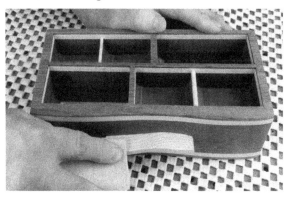

Finish up using the sponge sander.

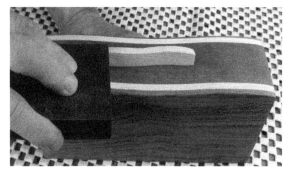

Insert the drawer in your box and they are now ready for staining.

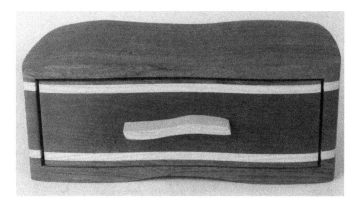

95

Sample Handle Patterns are for examples, use these or create your own. Finished handle depth should be a minimum of 1/2 to 3/4". Handle thickness can be as slim as 3/16" but 1/4" works well.

Some of the patterns below are near a useable size for your box drawers, others are oversized to allow you to see the shaping and will need to be reduced to fit your drawers.

Stretch a handle pattern for a larger drawer. Reduce the length for a smaller drawer keeping the depth and the thickness consistent.

Simply reversing a pattern gives a different look.

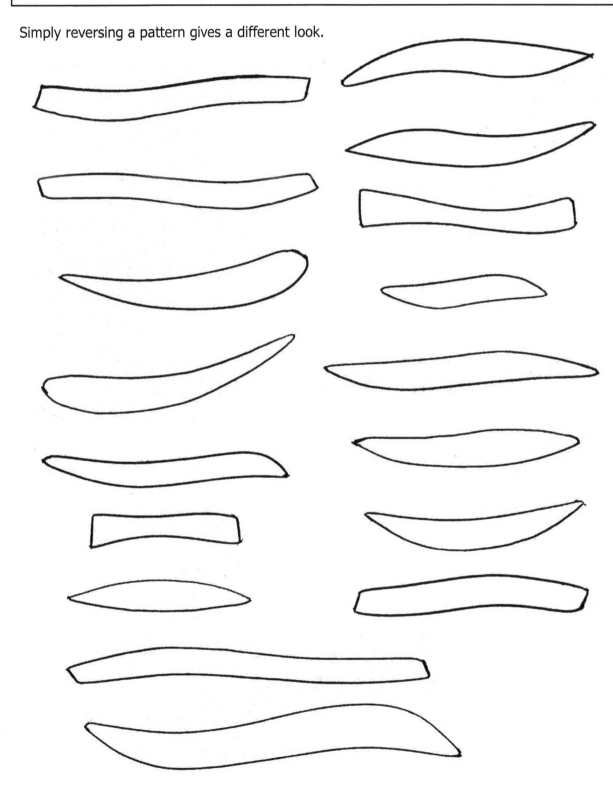

Chapter 14- Finishing

Finishing your box is an individual decision. Every woodworking book that I've read seems to have their own version of what they believe is the ideal finish to use. That is subjective. What works for them might not work for you.

The best finish to use is one that enhances the appearance of your project, is durable, one that will give you a great finish for many years to come, but most importantly one in which you feel comfortable applying.

What kind of finish do you have on your boxes? I wish that I had a quarter for every time that I have answered that question.

I start by finish sanding to 180 grit. I use an oil stain, either a medium to dark walnut or natural stain depending on the type of wood. A clear or natural stain works well on woods like walnut, ash, maple and wenge where you want the natural color of the wood to be shown. It makes woods like bloodwood and padauk "pop".

A medium walnut stain is used to darken oak.

Before applying my finish, I do a light sanding with a 320 grit or higher paper to smooth out any raised grain areas. You can find some great thin sponge pads with higher grits that cater to the automotive industry, but they also work well for wood, at many paint stores.

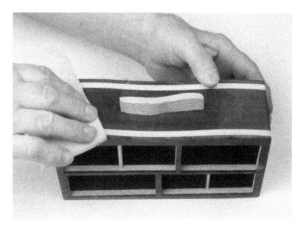

Always use a tack cloth after any sanding and right before you apply your finish.

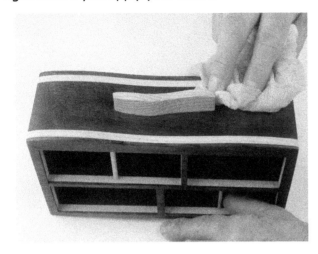

I follow that by spraying a coat of lacquer sanding sealer. The box and drawers are then sanded again with a very fine sanding sponge gives you an incredibly smooth finish.

Several coats of a satin nitrocellulose lacquer are then sprayed on followed by a buffed paste wax.

I have used this process for years and it has worked out well for me. The lacquer levels out nicely and subsequent coats melt and blend together creating a smooth brush free finish.

Other options

One of the easiest finishes to use is an oil/varnish blend such as Watco Danish oil. Several coats of the oil following the manufacturer's guidelines will give you a natural feel to your wood. However it does offer very little scratch or water resistance. You can increase the durability by following the oil with a wipe on, brushed or sprayed polyurethane or lacquer.

A number of woodworkers make their own blend of finish such as using a mixture of boiled linseed oil, mineral spirits and polyurethane. I did that for awhile before I bought my HVLP spray system.

Odie's Oil is another product that many woodworkers are using today. It is a solvent free blend of oils and waxes that will leave your wood looking in a more natural state. All you need to do is rub a small amount on and buff.

You can read a lot more about finishes and finishing techniques in many articles or books. However, the best way to learn is to buy a few varieties of finish products and try the products your self on some prepared scrap wood and see how they work for you.

Flocking the Drawers

Most jewelry type boxes come with some kind of liner that enhances the appearance of the inside of the drawer. A plush velvet suede liner would be great, but it would be almost impossible to install in a band saw box.

Getting your drawers to look professionally finished has been made considerably easier over the years with the introduction of sprayed rayon fibers. Donjer (now just Flock It) has been one of the leaders in the small consumer market for over 65 years in providing flocking fibers.

Visit their website at www.flockit.com for product information.

Their fibers come in a wide arrange of colors and are easy to apply, however, I prefer to use a basic brown color to line the drawers as I want the box to stand out and not to be distracted by some bright color in the drawer.

Step 1 - The inside of your drawer where you will be applying the fibers needs to be sealed to prevent seepage of the adhesive, especially in porous woods like oak or ash. The flocking glue will seep through open grain woods to the outside of the drawer if not sealed.

Use a brushing lacquer, polyurethane or shellac on the bottom and sides of your drawer sections.

Step 2 - After your sealer has dried, you can apply the Suede-Tex adhesive in the drawer sections.

Use the adhesive color that corresponds to the color of the flocking that you will be using.

Apply a generous coat of adhesive. You will have a 10 to 15 minute working time.

Always recheck your drawer sections to make sure they are covered with enough adhesive before you go on to the next step.

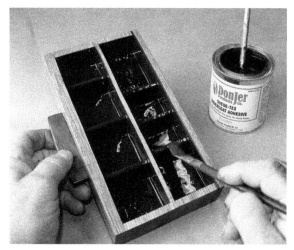

Some people tape off areas to catch adhesive drips. That is an unnecessarily time consuming thing to do. Keep a small amount of mineral spirits handy in a plastic container near by. Any drips can be easily wiped off using a paper towel dipped into the mineral spirits before you apply the flocking.

Step 3 - Fill your flocking tube or spray canister approximately 50% full. Spray the fibers at a distance of 8 to 10" at a downward angle.

Prop your drawer up on a block to get the angle that you need. Cover the bottom of the drawer first before moving to the sides.

Don't skimp, apply a very generous coating of fibers to the surface. Only so much will stick and the rest will fall off. Carefully set aside. Let dry at least 10 hours or overnight.

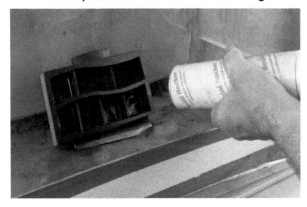

After drying, go back to your spraying box, turn your drawer upside down and shake out any loose fibers which can be reused.

> **Tip -** If you plan to do a lot of flocking, purchase a large clear plastic storage container for spraying into. Tape a cardboard stop a few inches high along the front and sides to help catch some of the fibers *(you won't be able to catch them all)*.
>
> The clear plastic will allow light to shine through. The excess fibers can be pushed to the side and used to refill your tube as you proceed from piece to piece.
>
> When finished, the fibers can easily be collected, the container vacuumed and it now becomes a storage box for your supplies.

Adding the Finishing Touches

Sign your completed box on the bottom.

Add protective pads.

Buff using a soft paste wax.

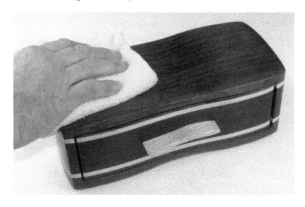

Take a step back to admire your completed project.

Appendix

Band Saw Box Building Quick Look Guide - the Basic Steps

1. Rip and crosscut your wood to size.
2. Glue up your wood into a solid block.
3. Square your block, smooth out at least the bottom.
4. Select and draw your pattern on your block or copy and paste a pattern on the block.
5. Set fence at 1/4", cut the back off of the block.
6. Cut out the drawer/s, set aside.
7. Glue the entry cut for a side drawer box,; or leave for a bottom cut box.
8. Sand lightly inside box cavity.
9. Glue on the back.
10. Cut your box profile.
11. Set fence at 1/4", cut off the back of the drawer/s.
12. Set fence at 3/8" to 1/2", cut off the front of the drawer/s.
13. Lay all pieces back into the box cavity.
14. Draw your drawer sections.
15. Cut out the drawer sections.
16. Sand lightly inside drawer sections.
17. Glue the drawer pieces back together.
18. Rough, then finish sand box and drawers.
19. Make a handle for the drawer and glue on.
20. Stain.
21. Apply finish.
22. Apply flocking.
23. Place protective pads on the bottom.
24. Sign the box.

These cover the basic steps for a traditional band saw box. Variations in designs, number of drawers, adding trays or mini-drawers will add greatly to the number of steps that will be needed to complete more involved boxes.

Common Mistakes
And Troubleshooting

The most common mistake is not marking a reference line across the top or side of the box, drawer, or hidden drawer after each cut to show the orientation causing an upside down cut or cutting the wrong width on the front or back piece. Unfortunately I still do that myself occasionally.

You've made your cut on your box profile and drawer and you've discovered that your wood has some hidden cracks or fissures.

Use a compatible wood filler to fill these before rough or finish sanding.

You can also use the wood filler to fill saw cuts that didn't close up completely after gluing.

Did you sand the drawer to much leaving a larger gap at the top of your drawer opening?

Adding a couple of strips of sticky felt to the bottom of the drawer may solve the problem.

Accidents happen, like this top section breaking off from its support. Luckily it's wood, so glue it back together. The side pieces will add support to be just like the original.

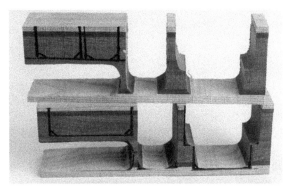

Add felt pads to the back of your drawer if it sets to far back in your drawer cavity due to the extra middle saw cuts.

Two drawer box templates - *If you plan to be making a lot of boxes similar to the contemporary ones, then drawing up a template will help you save a lot of time with your layout.*

I have a template for the Two drawer small bottom boxes and one for the Two drawer large bottom boxes. What is nice about the Two drawer large bottom template is that it can also be used when laying out the dimensions on the one drawer boxes too.

Two drawer large bottom template with suggested dimensions.

The drawer size on the template is drawn at the minimum size of 2 1/2" for the bottom drawer and 1/ 1/4" for the top drawer.

To use, lay the base of the template next to the bottom of your box block, draw a line corresponding to the bottom and the top of the drawers.

Adjust the size of the drawers by sliding the template either up and down along the drawer section to increase or decrease the size of the drawer and to allow for thc 3/8 1/2" middle divide between the drawers.

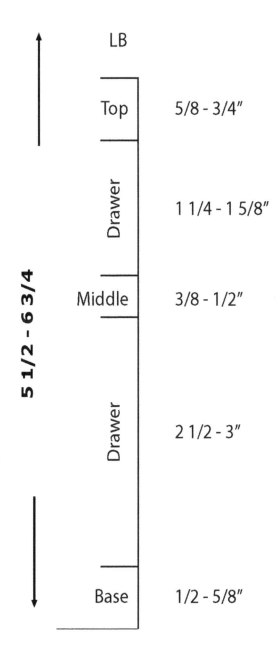

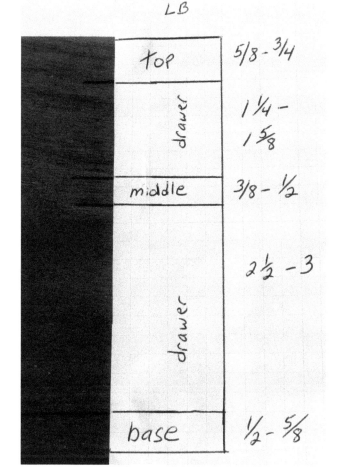

not to size.

Use either your square or your ruler gauge to draw out your layout lines.

Two drawer small bottom template with suggested dimensions.

SB

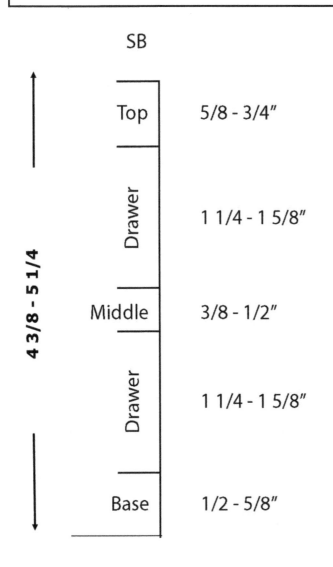

Top	5/8 - 3/4"
Drawer	1 1/4 - 1 5/8"
Middle	3/8 - 1/2"
Drawer	1 1/4 - 1 5/8"
Base	1/2 - 5/8"

4 3/8 - 5 1/4

not to size.

Small basic box

- 2 pieces 1/2" walnut
- 2 pieces 7/8" oak
- 1 piece 1/8" padauk

Cut at 5 1/2 x 3"

Prepared block size
- 5 x 2 7/8 x 2 3/4"

Final size, ready for finishing.
- 4 1/2 x 2 5/8 x 2 3/4"

Small basic box with tray, side or back mini - drawer

- 1 piece 5/8" oak glue up
- 3 pieces 7/8" oak
- 1 piece 1/8" padauk
- 1 piece 1/32" black veneer

Cut at 7 1/2 x 4 1/4"

Prepared block size
- 7 x 4 x 3 1/2"

Final size, ready for finishing.
- 6 x 3 3/4 x 3 1/2"

Small contemporary box with side or back mini - drawer

- 2 pieces 7/8" walnut
- 2 pieces 1 1/8" ash
- 1 piece 1/32" black veneer

Cut at 7 1/4 x 4 1/4"

Prepared block size
- 7 x 4 x 3 3/4"

Final size, ready for finishing.
- 6 5/8 x 3 5/8 x 3 3/4"

Medium contemporary non-divided drawer box

- 1 piece 1/2" walnut glue up
- 1 piece 1 1/8" walnut
- 2 pieces 7/8" walnut
- 1 piece 1/8" padauk
- 2 pieces 1/32" black veneer

Cut at 9 x 4 x 4"

Prepared block size

- 8 1/2 x 3 7/8 x 4"

Final size, ready for finishing.

- 8 x 3 1/2 x 4"

Large contemporary divided drawer curved front and back box

- 2 pieces 7/8" bubinga
- 2 pieces 1/4" maple
- 1 piece 1 3/4" walnut

Cut at 11 1/2 x 5 1/4"

Prepared block size

- 11 x 4 x 5"

Final size, ready for finishing.

- 10 1/2 x 3 3/4 x 4 7/8"

Side by side divided drawer box

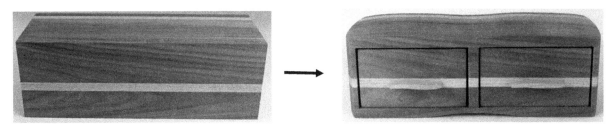

- 1 piece 5/8" walnut glue up
- 1 pieces 1/2" honey locust
- 1 piece 1/2" walnut
- 2 pieces 1 1/8" walnut

Cut at 13 1/2 x 4 1/2"

Prepared block size

- 13 x 4 1/4 x 4"

Final size, ready for finishing.

- 12 1/2 x 4 x 4"

Two drawer small bottom drawer flat front and back box

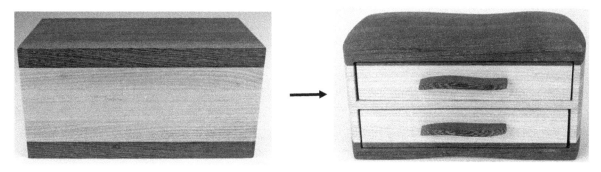

- 2 pieces 7/8" wenge
- 3 pieces 1 1/8" ash

Cut at 10 1/2 x 5 1/4"

Prepared block size
- 10 x 5 x 5 "

Final size, ready for finishing.
- 9 3/4 x 4 1/2 x 5"

Two drawer large bottom drawer curved front and back box

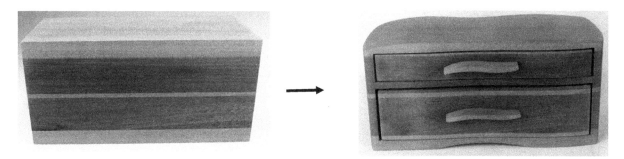

- 2 pieces 3/4" sapele
- 1 piece 1/4" sapele
- 2 pieces 1 3/4" walnut

Cut at 12 x 5 3/4"

Prepared block size
- 11 1/2 x 5 1/2 x 5"

Final size, ready for finishing.
- 11 x 5 x 4 3/4"

Tower box

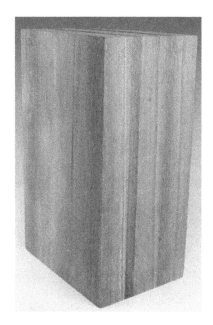

- 3 pieces 1 1/4" walnut
- 2 pieces 1/2" blood-wood

Cut at 11 1/2 x 6 3/4"

Prepared block size
- 6 1/2 x 11 1/2 x 4 3/4"

Final size, ready for finishing.
- 6 1/4 x 11 x 4 3/4"

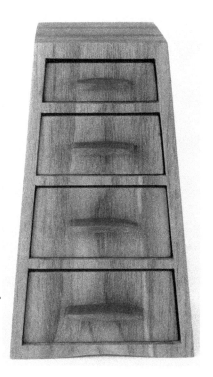

Patterns

This chapter contains sample patterns of most of the box designs shown in this book.

* There is a diagram of the basic box profile with suggested dimensions.

* There are several examples of drawer patterns that will compliment the box. Add more sections for use with little things; make larger sections for watches, beads or chains. There are a countless number of variations that can be made.

* Split the drawer for a wider box, eliminate the middle divider for a narrower box.

* The contemporary box designs will also include a top view look into the box from above to show several of the pull out mini-drawers.

* The patterns are not drawn to size. Either enlarge or reduce the pattern to fit the block size that you have made.

* Experiment with wood combinations to make your box stand out.

* Refer back to the earlier chapters for more detailed instructions if needed.

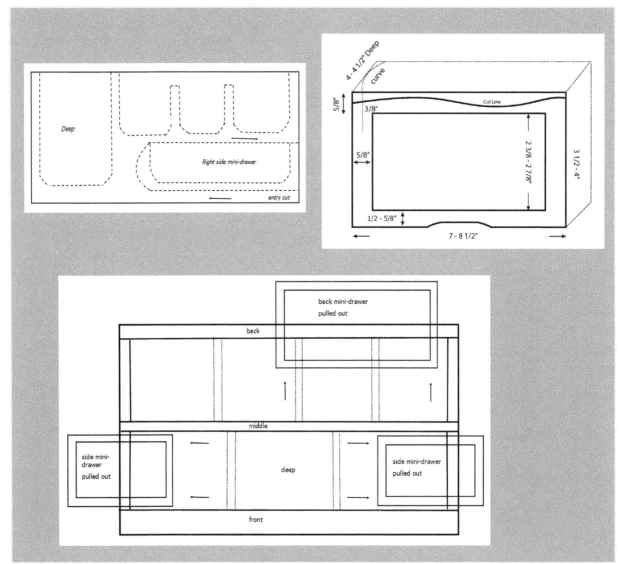

Traditional box basic patterns - *These diagrams are suggestions as to what a traditional band saw box drawer pattern can look like. They are used for reference. Plans can be enlarged or reduced on a copy machine to match your box block.*

Bottom entry cut - one section- Start entry cut at the box bottom, back the blade out.

Do not glue entry cut closed after cutting out the drawer, sand cut open edge to soften.

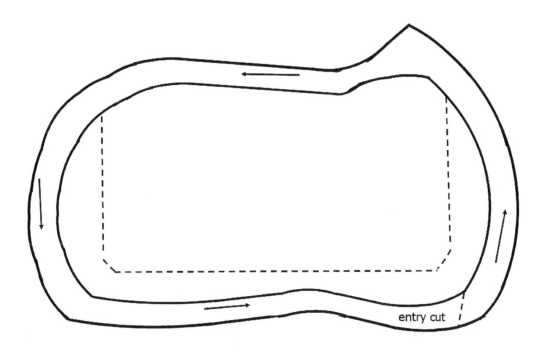

entry cut

Bottom entry cut - two sections - Start entry cut at the box bottom, back the blade out.

Do not glue entry cut closed after cutting out the drawer, sand cut open edge to soften.

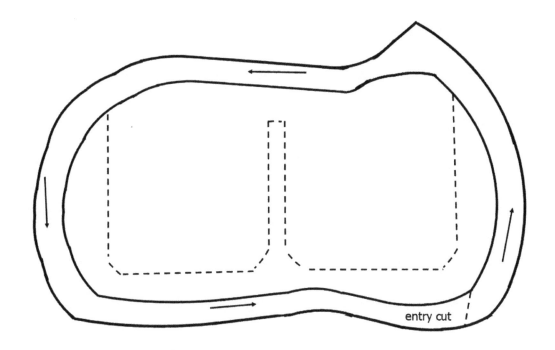

entry cut

109

Side entry cut - one section - Start entry cut at the box side, back the blade out.
Glue entry cut closed after cutting out the drawer.

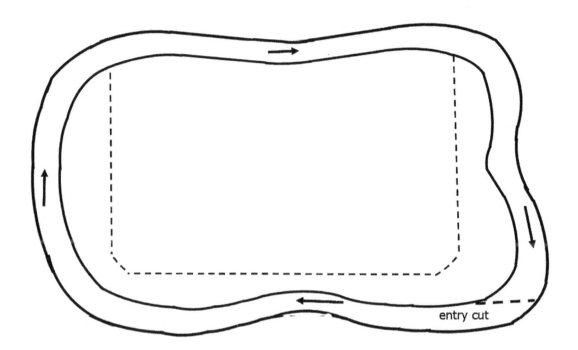

entry cut

Side entry cut - two sections - Start entry cut at the box side, back the blade out.
Glue entry cut closed after cutting out the drawer.

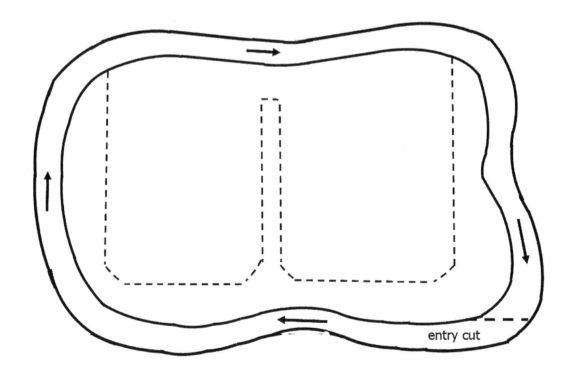

entry cut

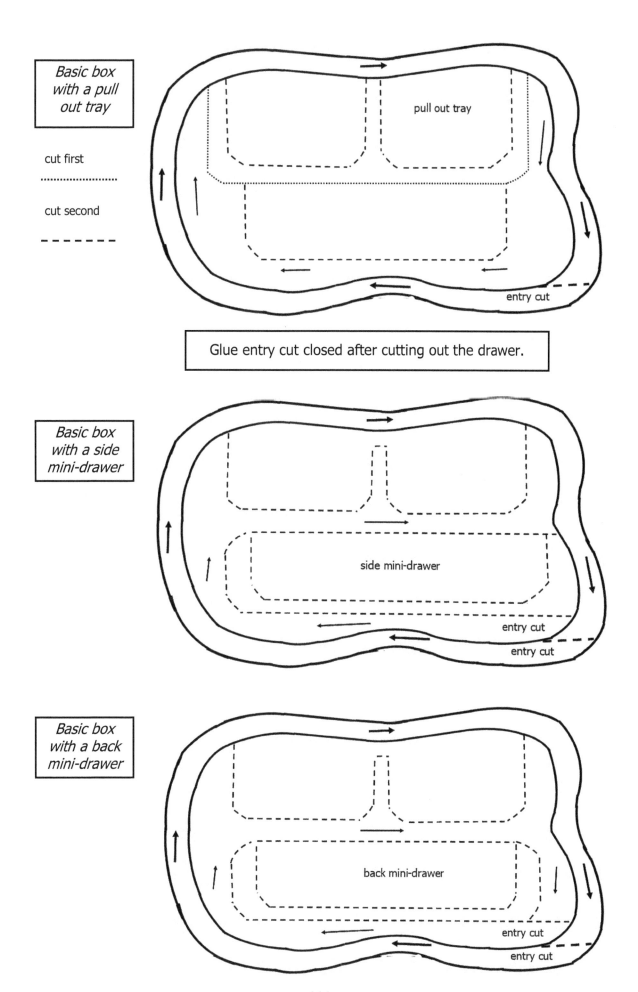

Basic box with a pull out tray

cut first

....

cut second

– – – – – –

pull out tray

entry cut

Glue entry cut closed after cutting out the drawer.

Basic box with a side mini-drawer

side mini-drawer

entry cut

entry cut

Basic box with a back mini-drawer

back mini-drawer

entry cut

entry cut

Basic Contemporary Box Profile - *as drawn not to size, increase or decrease box size from 6 to 6 1/2 inches in length along with suggested width and height measurements.*

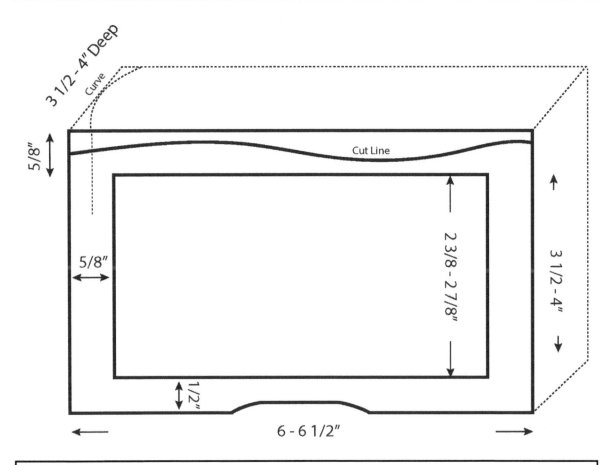

Sample drawer section with a left side mini-drawer is for an example and is not drawn to size. The drawer could also be made with the mini-drawer pulled to open on the right side.

Start entry cut at the mini-drawer bottom exiting out the top side.

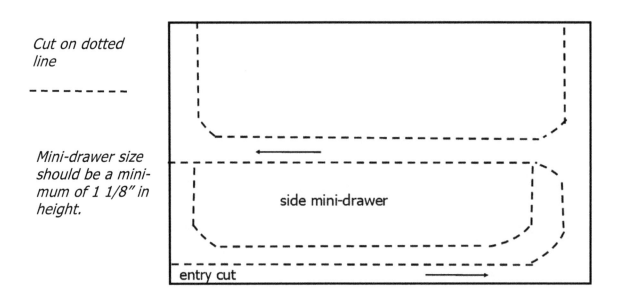

Cut on dotted line

- - - - - - - -

Mini-drawer size should be a minimum of 1 1/8" in height.

Top view looking down into **Basic Contemporary Box Drawer,** single section on upper layer with back mini-drawer pulled out on bottom layer (not to size).

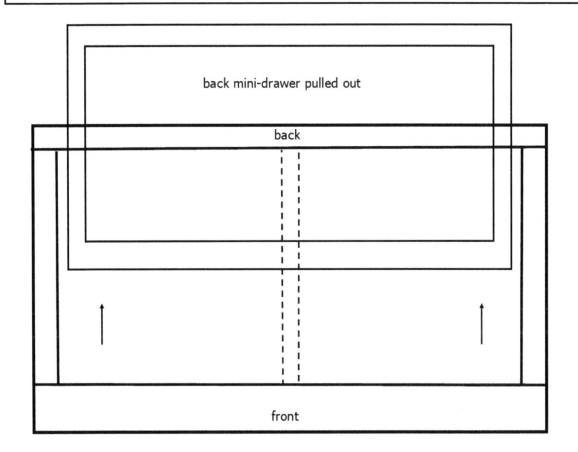

back mini-drawer pulled out

back

front

Sample drawer section with a back mini-drawer is an example and is not drawn to size.

Cut on dotted line

- - - - - - - -

Mini-drawer size should be a minimum of 1 1/8" in height.

Glue entry cut closed after cutting out the back mini-drawer.

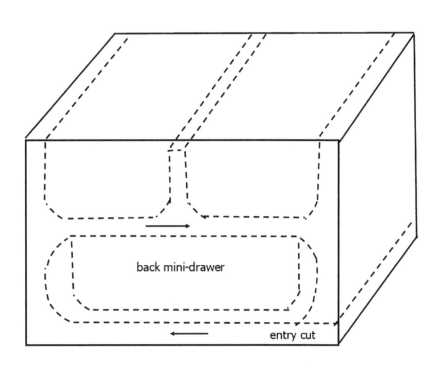

back mini-drawer

entry cut

Top view looking down into **Basic Contemporary Box Drawer,** single section on upper layer with a right side mini-drawer pulled out on bottom layer (not to size).

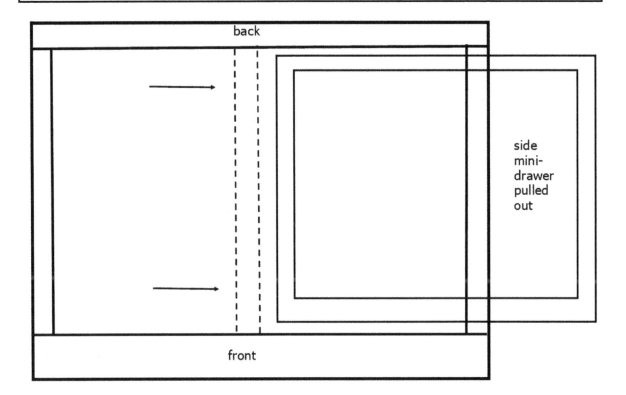

Sample drawer section with a right side mini-drawer is for an example and is not drawn to size. The drawer could also be made with the mini-drawer pulled to open on the left side.

Cut on dot-
ted line

Mini-drawer
size should
be a mini-
mum of 1
1/8" in

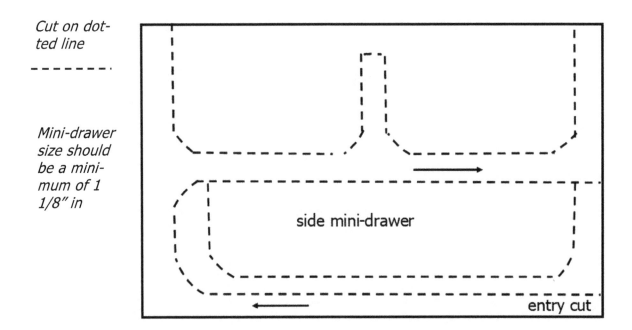

side mini-drawer

entry cut

Medium Contemporary Box Profile - *as drawn not to size, increase or decrease box size from 7 to 8 1/2 inches in length along with suggested width and height measurements.*

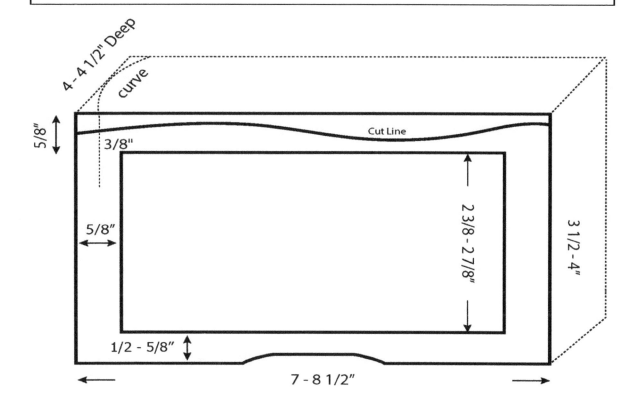

Sample drawer section for the **Medium Contemporary Box** with a back mini-drawer is an example and is not drawn to size, add or adjust the sections to fit your drawer block.

Start entry cut at the side for a back mini-drawer, then back out the blade, glue entry cut closed.

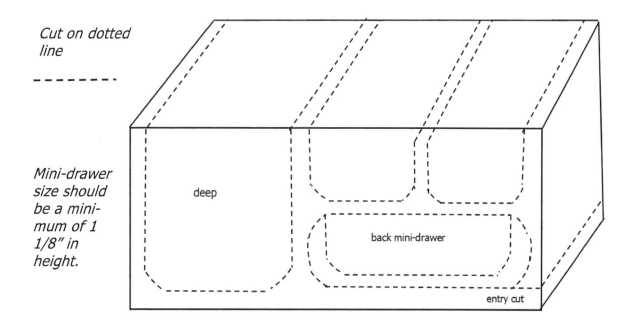

Top view of drawer insert from the previous page.

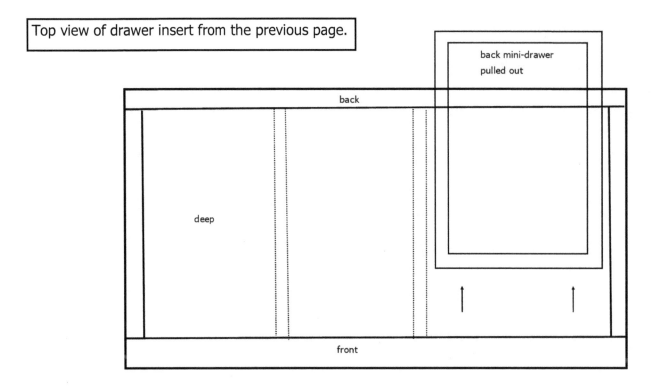

Additional drawer patterns for the **Medium Contemporary Box** with a side mini-drawer on each side of the box; or a back/side mini-drawer combination.

Start entry cut at the drawer bottom for a side mini-drawer exiting out the side.

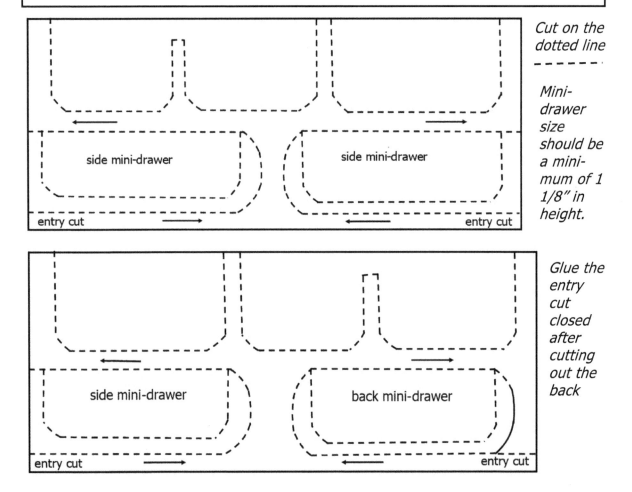

Cut on the dotted line

- - - - - -

Mini-drawer size should be a mini-mum of 1 1/8" in height.

Glue the entry cut closed after cutting out the back

Large Contemporary Split Drawer Box Profile - *as drawn not to size, increase or decrease box size from 8 to 12 inches in length along with suggested width and height measurements.*

Split the drawer for a deeper box, eliminate the middle divider for a narrower box.

See next pages for various combinations.

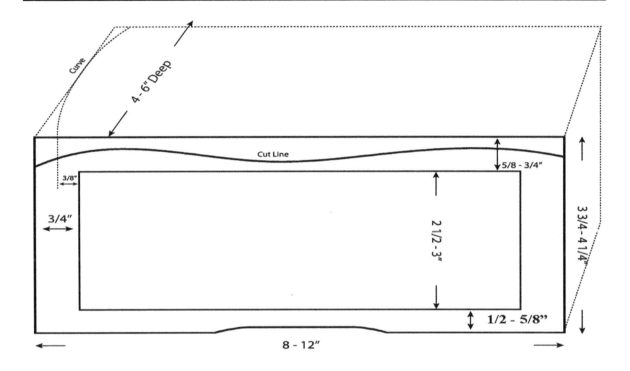

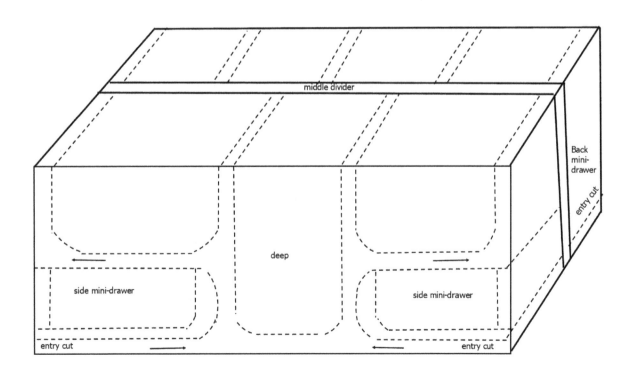

Top view looking down into a **Large Contemporary Divided Drawer Box,** *several sections on upper layer with a back mini-drawer pulled out on bottom back layer and left and right side mini-drawers on the front section (not to size).* Patterns follow the top view look.

Sections with a back mini-drawer will need to be placed on the back half of the drawer.

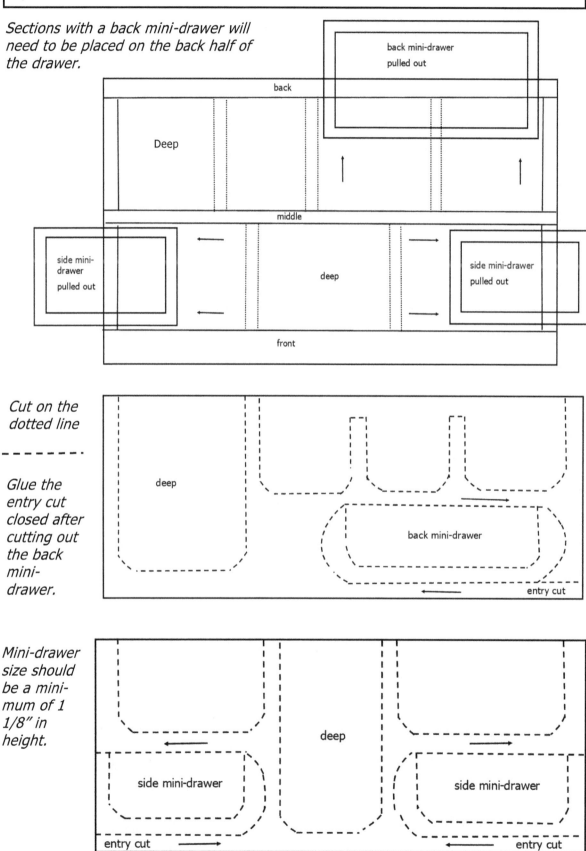

Cut on the dotted line

- - - - - - -

Glue the entry cut closed after cutting out the back mini-drawer.

Mini-drawer size should be a minimum of 1 1/8" in height.

*Top view looking down into a **Large Contemporary Divided Drawer Box**, several sections on upper layer with back mini-drawer pulled out on bottom back layer and a left side mini-drawer on the front section (not to size). Patterns follow the top view look.*

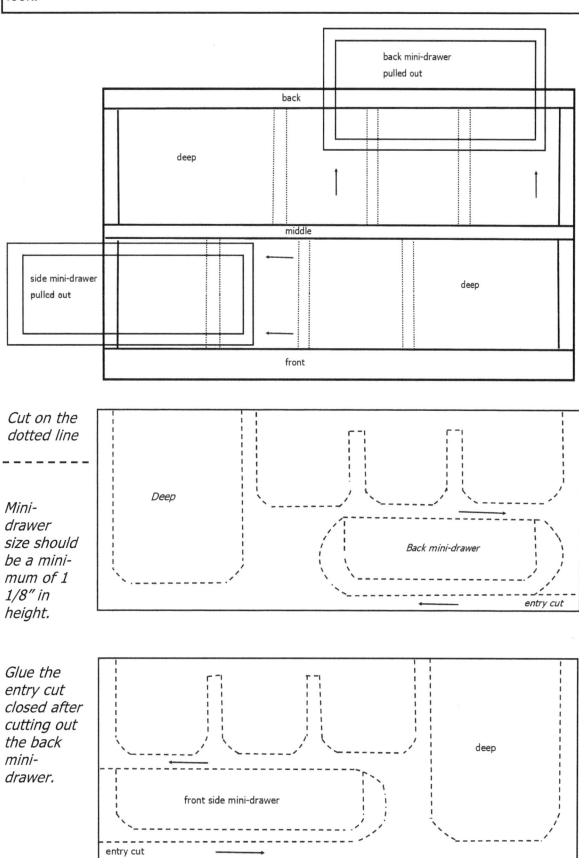

back mini-drawer
pulled out

back

deep

middle

side mini-drawer
pulled out

deep

front

Cut on the
dotted line

Mini-drawer size should be a minimum of 1 1/8" in height.

Deep

Back mini-drawer

entry cut

Glue the entry cut closed after cutting out the back mini-drawer.

front side mini-drawer

deep

entry cut

Top view looking down into a **Large Contemporary Divided Drawer Box,** several sections on upper layer with a left side mini-drawer on the front section and a right side mini-drawer on the back section (not to size). Patterns follow the top view look.

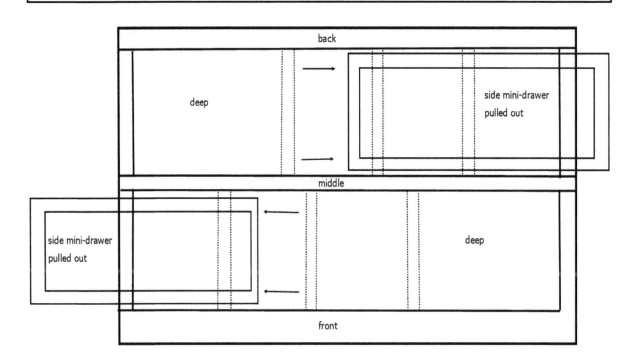

Cut on the dotted line

- - - - - - -

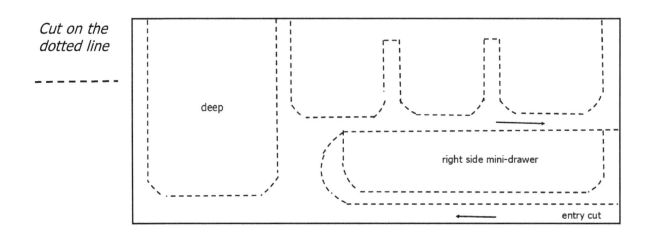

Mini-drawer size should be a minimum of 1 1/8" in height.

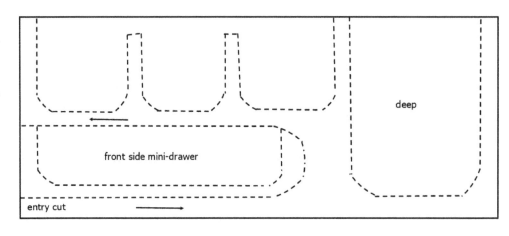

Top view looking down into a **Large Contemporary Divided Drawer Box**, several sections on upper layer with left and right side mini-drawers on the front section and a right side mini-drawer on the back section (not to size). Patterns follow the top view look.

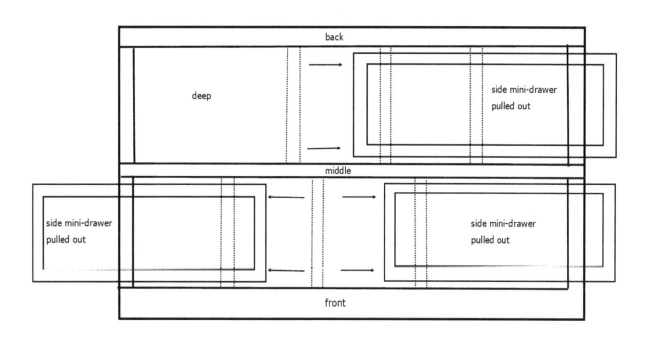

Cut on the dotted line

- - - - -

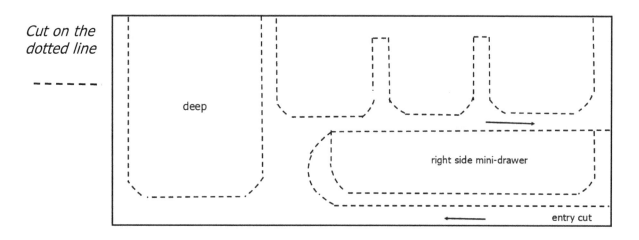

Mini-drawer size should be a minimum of 1 1/8" in height.

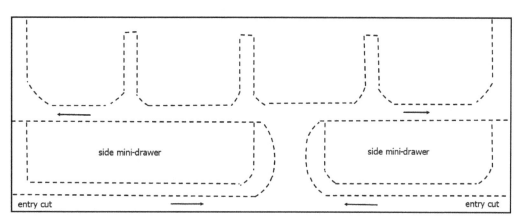

Two Drawer Small Bottom Box Profile - *as drawn not to size, increase or decrease box size from 10 to 12 inches in length along with suggested width and height measurements.*

Split the drawer for a wider box, eliminate the middle divider for a narrower box.

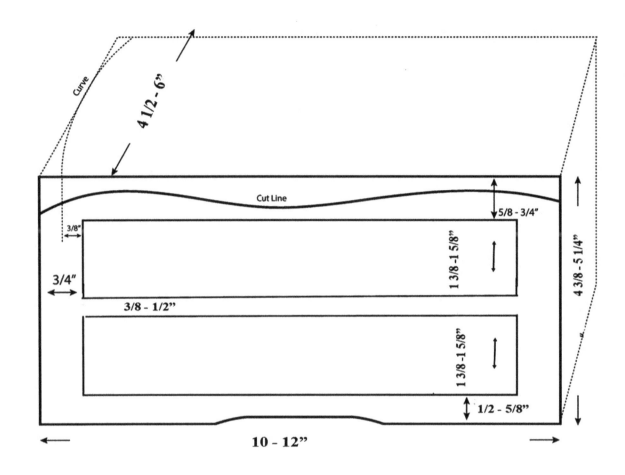

Use a combination of the single drawer patterns (more on the next page) to allow the box to be more versatile for different sizes of items.

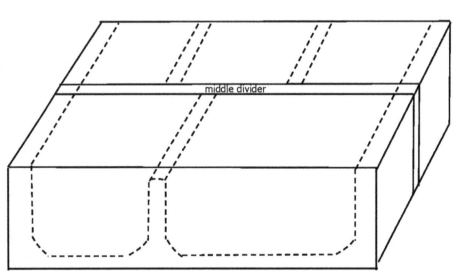

Additional drawer patterns for the **Top on Top Small Drawer Boxes.** Use these for examples, make any changes to fit the needs of your box drawer.

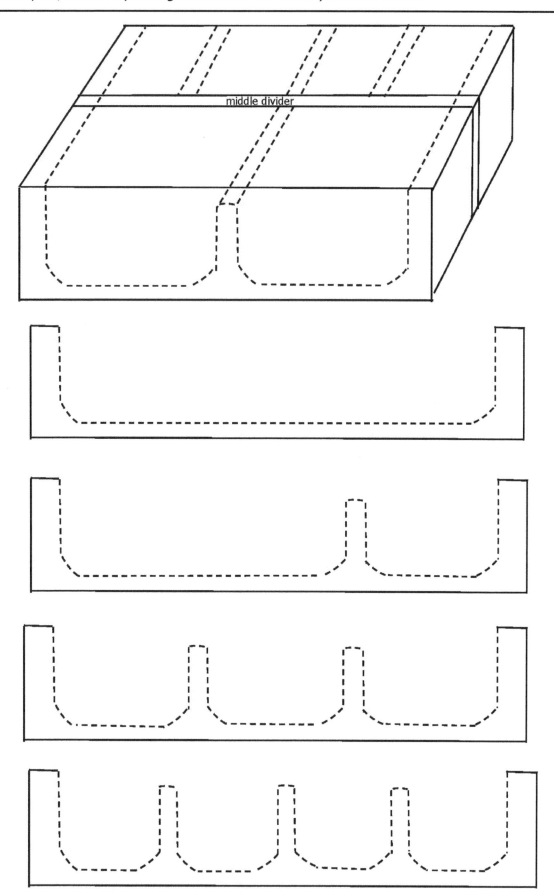

middle divider

Two Drawer Large Bottom Box Profile - *as drawn not to size, increase or decrease box size from 10 to 12 inches in length along with suggested width and height measurements.*

Split the drawer for a wider box, eliminate the middle divider for a narrower box.

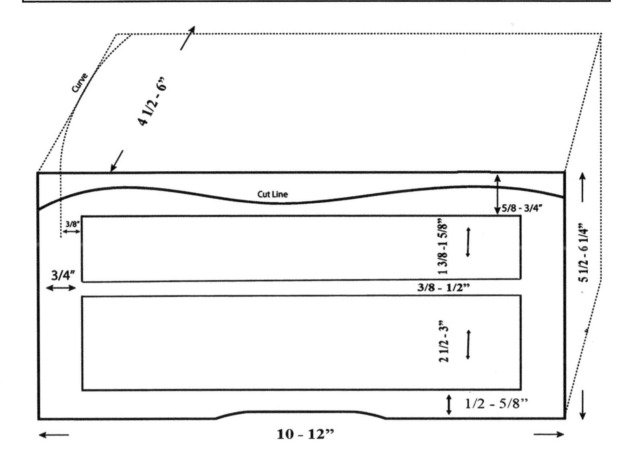

Place a small drawer on the top and a large drawer with pull out mini-drawers on the bottom.

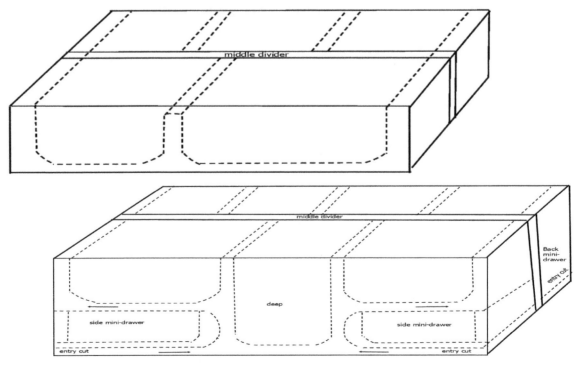

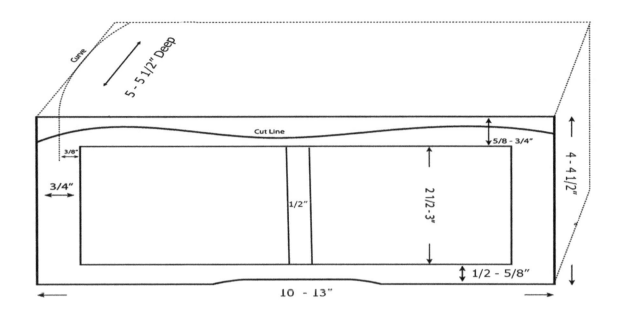

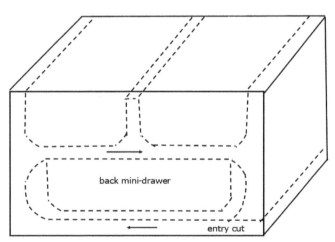

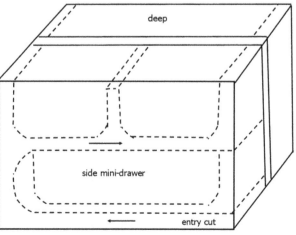

Tower Box Profile - *as drawn not to size, measurements are suggested. Increase or decrease to fit your box block. Adding additional height will allow for a fifth drawer.*

See next pages for drawer patterns.

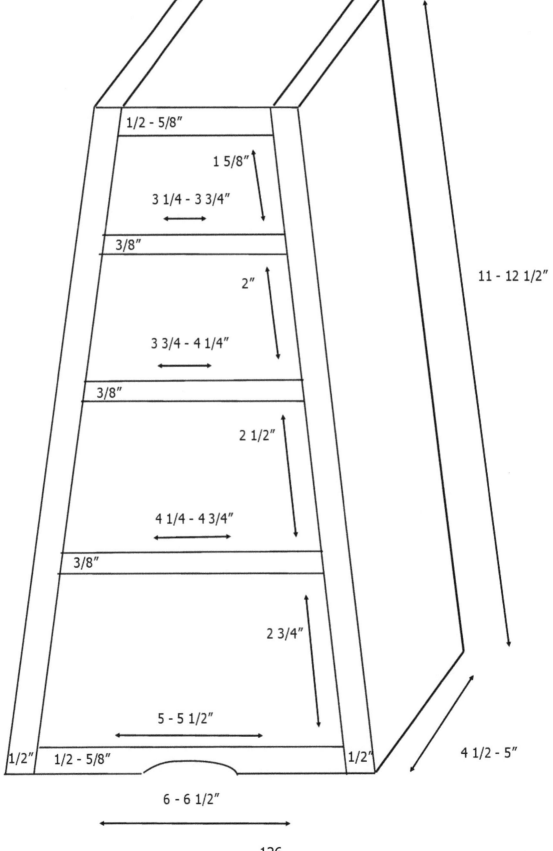

The bottom drawer is a split drawer with a side mini-drawer in the front and a back mini-drawer in the back half of the drawer.

Bottom drawer front half

Bottom drawer back half

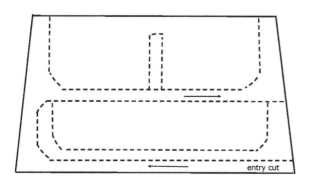

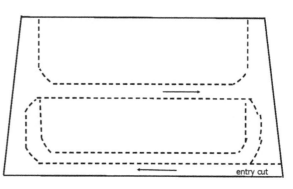

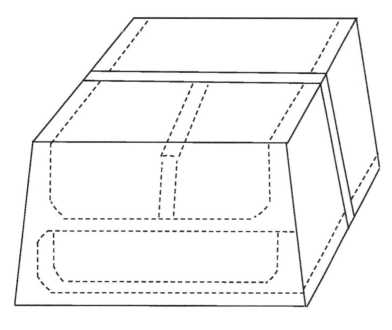

Glue back mini-drawer entrance cut closed.

The second drawer is a split drawer with a side mini-drawer in the front and a deep section in the back half of the drawer.

Second drawer front half

Second drawer back half

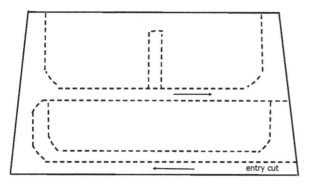

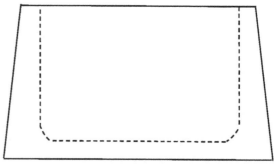

The third drawer from the bottom is a single open section.

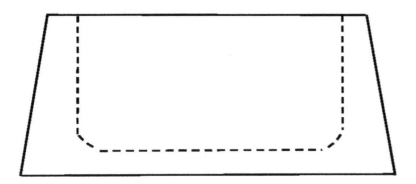

Large section for a watch, bracelet, beads, chain or other larger item.

The top drawer is a split drawer with a side larger section in the front and a split section in the back half of the drawer. Sections can be switched.

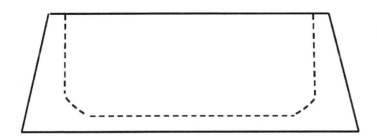

Top drawer front half

Top drawer back half

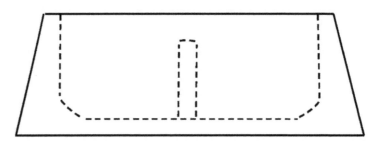

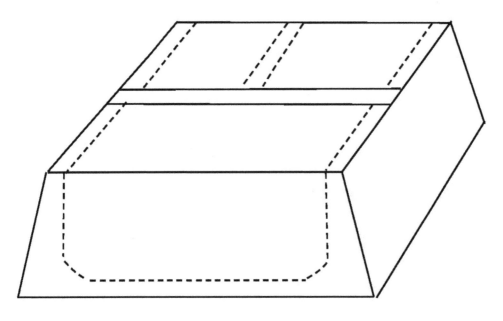

Copy the pattern and use as is for a smaller box.

Enlarge the size to 115 - 120% or more for a larger box.

Gallery

Sapele and ash

10″ L x 4 1/2″H x 5″ D

Wenge and white oak

11″ L x 5 1/4″H x 5″ D

Walnut and purpleheart

9" L x 4 1/2"H x 4" D

White oak, bloodwood, padauk with black veneer

8 1/2" L x 4 1/2"H x 4" D

Walnut and ash

8" L x 4 1/2"H x 4" D

Sapele and ash
10″ L x 4″H x 5″ D

Walnut and ash
12″ L x 5″H x 5″ D

Walnut and ash
with black veneer

8″ L x 4″H x 4″ D

Walnut, ash and
white veneer

10" L x 4 1/2"H x 4" D

White oak and bloodwood

6" L x 3 1/2"H x 3 1/2" D

Sapele, white oak and black veneer

10 1/2"L x 4"H x 5" D

Bubinga, walnut and ash

10 1/2" L x 3 3/4"H x 4 3/4" D

White oak and padauk

10 1/2"L x 4"H x 5" D

Sapele and wenge

12 1/2″ H x 6″W x 4 1/2″ D

White oak, padauk with
black veneer

61/2″ L x 3 1/2″H x 3 1/2″ D

Printed in the USA
CPSIA information can be obtained
at www.ICGtesting.com
LVHW071940110224
771549LV00013B/44